365 Creative Party Ideas

For All Ages

By Sheila Ellison and Nancy Maley

Forward March™ Press
Redwood City, CA

Published By:
Forward March™ Press
831 Sweeney Ave., Suite G
Redwood City, CA 94063-3028 (415) 366-0708

First Printing Oct. 1991

ISBN# 0-9620467-7-9

U.S. Booksellers Distributor: Publishers Group West 1-800-788-3123

Cover drawing by: Jay Ritchey

Printed in the United States of America

Dedication

In gratitude to my parents,
Tom and Elizabeth,
family and friends who have
entered into celebration with
the Maley Family —
Dave, Susan and Dale,
Sheila and Riki, Karen,
David, Brian and Brennen.

Keep the party alive!

– Nancy

To my father,
who has always had
time in his life for fun,
and compassion in his
heart for others.

– Sheila

Introduction by the Authors

There is an old saying, "Life is what you make of it!" The celebrations we give ourselves and others can be a source of joy in our lives and in the lives of others. Everyone remembers special moments and celebrations. Parties can create family traditions and rituals which will be passed down with love.

It is important for people to feel special, to be honored, to have their own day. This book is about making life what you want it to be. It is full of ideas to bring hours of fun and togetherness to your celebrations. It might even give you reasons to celebrate that you never thought of before!

This book contains 17 chapters including: Holidays, Wedding Showers, American Tradition, Birthday Parties from Preschool to Adult, Housewarming and Neighborhood Parties, Free at Last! Retirement Parties, Fundraisers, and more! Also included is a party planning chapter which gives you general advice about scheduling parties, party helpers, using locations outside the home, in restaurants, etc. It also contains suggestions for specific age groups of kids parties.

Menu ideas are listed but we have excluded recipes as there are a large number of good cookbooks available. Many parties can be used in more than one category. The important thing is to take the idea offered, be creative, and make it your own! Don't be afraid to put love and energy into your parties. They may be the moments in life that will be remembered forever!

Table of Contents

Marching Band Party

Invitations
- Send invitations made in the shape of a drum or horn.
- Ask children to bring a musical instrument.

Decorations
Decorate party room with musical notes, record covers, and streamers.

Activities
- Make drums out of oatmeal boxes. Decorate with paper and crayons.
- Create wrist bells by sewing small bells onto a ribbon. Wrap around wrist and tie into a bow.
- Before opening presents and eating, have birthday child lead guests around house and neighborhood in a musical parade.

1

Circus Fun

Invitations
- Blow up a balloon and write invitation with permanent felt tip pen (do not tie).
- Send a note with balloon telling guests to blow it up for party information.

Decorations
- Decorate room with balloons and crepe paper.
- If your budget allows, hire a clown, mime, magician, or facepainter.

Activities

- Pretend the party is a carnival and have different games going simultaneously.
- Rehearse a circus show and perform for parents when they arrive to pick children up.

Menu
Food you might find at a circus is appropriate, for example, hot dogs, peanuts, caramel corn, ice cream, etc. Serve food from a "make-believe" concession stand.

2

Un-Birthday Party

Invitations
- Attach party information to back of a playing card.
- Ask guests to wear a crazy party hat.

Decorations
Use "Alice in Wonderland" for your theme. Make huge playing cards on butcher paper.

Activities
- Play follow the leader. Leader should dance, hop, skip, etc.
- Sing "Happy Un-Birthday!" Put candles on cake and let each guest blow one out, while adding another, until everyone has had a chance to blow them out.

Menu
Serve tea and cupcakes.

3

Paper Party

Decorations
- Hang paper chains, paper flowers, paper birds, and paper streamers.
- Serve food on paper plates.
- Favors might be paper dolls, storybooks, coloring books, etc.

Activities
- Make paper hats.
- Draw outline of each child on a piece of butcher paper and let them "color themselves."
- Have a picture parade for parents when they arrive to pick children up.

4

Bears on Parade

Invitations
- Make or buy an invitation with bears on it. Cut invitation into 5-7 puzzle-like pieces.
- Encourage guests to bring their favorite teddy bear.

Decorations
Decorate house with stuffed bears and other animals you may have. If party is held outdoors, hide stuffed animals in trees or bushes.

Activities
- Let children dress up and have a parade with teddy bears.
- Tell bear stories. Sit in a circle and let children take turns telling about what their bears like to do, and why they like their bears.
- Have a teddy graham cookie hunt. Hide cookies around house and yard and let children find them.

5

Balls, Balls, and More Balls

This is a perfect party for toddlers.

Decorations
- Borrow as many balls as possible and place in baskets around the party area.
- Hang colorful balloons.

Activities
- Each child should have a ball to roll on grass while following a leader.
- Throw balls into a basket.
- Throw balls into a plastic pool to make splashes in the water.

Menu
- Cut sandwiches into circular shapes.
- Serve ice cream balls, fruit balls, cheese balls, etc.

6

Car and Truck Party

Invitations
- Cut out shapes of cars and trucks with construction paper.
- Ask each child to bring favorite riding car and little car.

Decorations
- Make traffic lights, cars, trucks, stop signs, etc.
- Use primary colored balloons.

Activities
- Obstacle Course: Have the birthday child help construct an obstacle course. Time each contestant as they maneuver through the course. Award each child with a "safe driver" ribbon.
- City on Wheels: Put a long piece of butcher paper on the floor and draw roads, railroad tracks, and city locations. When the city is completed, have children "drive" their small cars through it.

7

A is for Alphabet

For preschool ages to 7 years.

Invitations
Make a card in the shape of the letter that begins the birthday child's name.

Decorations
Cut out large letters from colored cardboard. The letters can be stapled to sticks and put into the ground for creating an alphabet path, or used for wall hangings.

Activities
- Guessing Game: Fill a large bag with different items. Pull an item out and have children tell you what letter it begins with.
- People Alphabet: Form groups of 2-4. Make letters on floor with bodies!

Menu
Serve alphabet soup and a letter-shaped cake or cupcakes decorated with different letters. Encourage children to create alphabet food sculptures with bowls of pretzels, carrot and celery sticks, etc. and a bowl of cream cheese.

8

My Favorite Characters

Decorations
Decorate party area with birthday kids favorite TV characters dolls, books, puppets, etc.

Activities
- String Hunt: Before children arrive, cut 40-50 lengths (in different sizes) of twine. Hide the string around the room. Play theme music while children find the segments. When the time allotment is up, line up each child's string to measure total length. This is fun since the number found does not necessarily determine the winner!
- Dance: Play theme tape and have children dance. Adult turns off the music and everyone must freeze. Do this until children are tired of game!

9

Puppet Party

- You will need to have a few parents or helpers in attendance at this party!
- Collect old socks, scraps of fabrics, buttons, glue, and yarn. Make a puppet stage out of an old refrigerator box. As children arrive, have someone read different storybooks to give children an idea of who they want their puppets to be. When everyone has arrived, start creating the puppets!
- Give each child the chance to perform a puppet show on the stage, either individually or in groups. You may want to have an adult handling additional puppet characters to stimulate interaction.

10

Animal Age

Decorations
Decorate party area with pictures of animals. Play animal song records or tapes.

Activities
- Cover a lower wall with butcher paper. Have children draw their favorite animals.
- Animal Parade: Tell each child to pretend to be an animal and parade around the house.
- Animal Masks: Make masks of animals' faces with paper bags, crayons, construction paper, tape, pipe cleaners, yarn, etc.
- Animal Hunt: Hide plastic animals or animal crackers around party area.
- Animal Toss: Collect stuffed animals and toss into a laundry basket.

11

Sunshine Celebration

Invitations

Cut yellow-colored paper into shape of sun.

Decorations

Decorate party area with yellow balloons and yellow crepe paper. You may wish to hold party outdoors if you have a sandbox.

Activities

- Sand City: Have children design and build a sand city together in a sandbox (or fill a wading pool with sand). Make sure there are plenty of props available.
- Pavement Painting: Let artists use paint brushes and buckets of water for painting designs on pavement or driveway. As the sun dries up the designs, make more!

Menu

Serve lunch in a sand bucket with a shovel and paint brush as the party favors.

12

Birthday for Valentines

Invitations
- Make valentines out of lace and colored construction paper. For fun, cut up valentines into puzzle pieces and let guests put them together to read party information. Or, put a picture of the birthday child in the center of the valentine.
- Ask guests to wear pink, red, or white.

Decorations
Decorate party area with red, pink, and white accessories.

Activities
- Decorate heart sugar cookies.
- Hide heart-shaped paper, lace, and other gluable items. Let children hunt and finally glue pieces to a large heart. When finished, give every child a prize.
- Make candy sculptures with marshmallows, toothpicks, gum drops, and jelly beans.

Menu
Serve a big heart cake and heart-shaped cookies.

13

Fairyland

Decorations

These can be anything imaginable - after all, it's fairyland! An idea might be to create a large cardboard rainbow with a foil-covered pot of gold at the end. For an outside party, stick large flowers, hearts, clouds, etc. made of heavy cardboard into the ground. You can also create a tunnel out of boxes and blankets. Hang foil stars and tinsel from the ceiling.

Activities

• Collect children's presents as they arrive. Throughout party as children are playing, place one present at a time in the pot of gold and ring a bell. The birthday child and guests will run over to see what is in the pot.

• Have 2' by 4' squares of fabric available to make fairy capes. Children can decorate with markers, paint, glitter, etc. Have children act out life in their fairyland with the capes and provided wands.

14

Beach Party

Children love the water and sand play, so why not invite them for a party where they can do just that!

Invitations
- Ask guests to wear bathing suits.
- It is dangerous to watch too many pre-schoolers in a pool, so use a hose, sprinkler, small plastic pool, and a sandbox.

Decorations
Place umbrellas, beach balls, and bright towels around party area.

Activities
- Make a water slide with a large piece of plastic.
- Have everyone help to make a town in the sandbox.
- Play games with a big beach ball.

Menu
Serve sandwiches, juice, oranges, and iced cupcakes.

15

Indian Pow-Wow

All children love to pretend to be Indians!

Invitations
• Send a note with a loose feather for child to wear to the party.
• Upon each child's arrival, make Indian outfits out of paper grocery bags. Have head and arms cut out beforehand and fringe bottoms. Let children decorate with yarn, crayons, etc.

Decorations
Decorate party area with feathers and balloons.

Activities
• Form in a circle and sing songs and dance. Have each child take a turn in leading others in a song and dance while staying in a circle.
• Make Indian headdresses.
• Go on a nature hike pretending to be Indians.

16

Flower Party

Invitations
- Write invitation on a package of flower seeds.
- Ask children to bring seeds to the party.
- Children should be dressed for outdoor play.

Decorations
- Decorate party area with large cardboard flowers.
- Decorate food items with real flowers (try to find edible flowers).

Activities
- Make flower face masks out of paper plates with center cut out. Glue colored flower petals to sides.
- Plant flower seeds in ground or in small containers for children to take home.
- Play a game which allows children to pretend to be nature items such as trees, rocks, flowers, birds, frogs, etc.

17

Animals on Parade

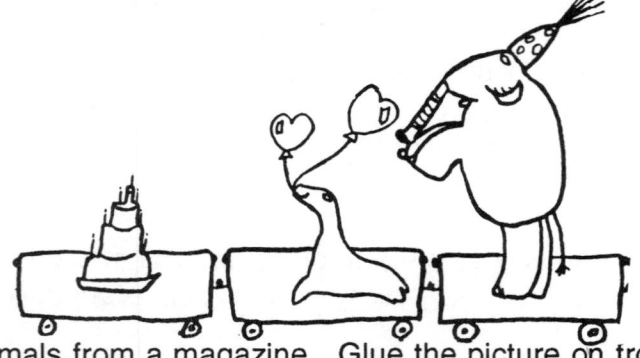

Invitations

Cut out pictures of animals from a magazine. Glue the picture on front of a card and write information inside. Children should bring their favorite pet. Announce that awards will be given.

Activities

As the children arrive with their pets, lead them to the backyard. If a child does not bring a pet, give them a judge's badge (make these ahead of time). Children should parade around the yard with their pets. Have enough awards to give one to each child. Give prizes for "longest tail," "cutest smile," "softest fur," "biggest feet," etc.

18

Dolls Tea Party

Invite a few friends over to celebrate your child's doll's birthday! Have the
guests bring their favorite dolls. Have each child tell a story about their doll.
Serve small tea sandwiches and petite cakes.

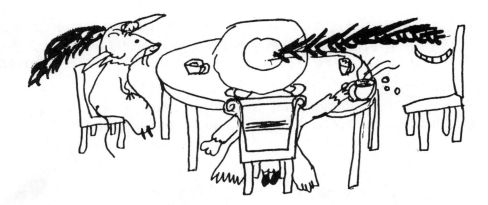

19

Mother Goose Party

Invitations

Make the invitation resemble a storybook with a goose on the front cover. Inside, choose a Mother Goose rhyme and insert party information.

Activities

- Have someone at the door dressed as a Mother Goose character who will read stories until all the guests have arrived.
- Ask children to act out nursery rhymes as an adult reads them aloud.
- Play "find the goose" by hiding a stuffed goose for guests to find.
- Cover a table with foil and make pat-a-cakes. Give each child a mound of shortbread batter, raisins, chocolate chips, sprinkles, etc. for decorations. Bake, and let children take them home.

20

Farm Fun

Invitations
- Cut invitation in the shape of a farm animal.
- Suggest the children wear overalls or jeans, straw hats, and bandanas.
- Have extra farmer props on hand so nobody feels left out.

Decorations
Decorate party area with clay bells, cornstalks, pumpkins, and a scarecrow.

Activities
- Color hard-boiled eggs.
- Call a local farm for pony rides.
- Plant beans (soaked overnight) in paper cups to take home.
- Arrange to go on a hayride.
- Try to "borrow" a bunny rabbit, baby pig, or other animals for children to touch and see.
- Have playdough available and animal-shaped cookie cutters.

21

Double Pleasure Twin Party

Everything at this party is done in duplicate.

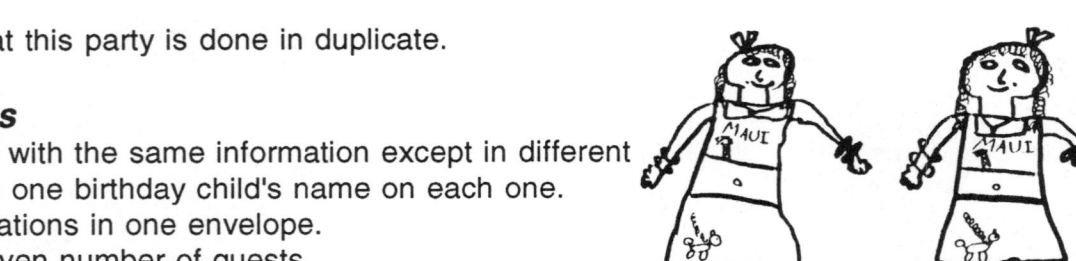

Invitations
- Two cards with the same information except in different colors with one birthday child's name on each one.
- Place invitations in one envelope.
- Invite an even number of guests.
- Have the party at 2:00.

Decorations
Have two cakes, two sets of decorations, place settings in two colors, and two selections of food.

Activities
- Play games that require teams of two. For example, wheelbarrow races, relay races with legs tied together, and face painting.

22

Who Will I Be?

Invitations
- Draw hats worn by policemen, firemen, and mail carriers on front of invitation.
- Request child to dress as either a policeman, a fireman, or a postman.

Decorations
Have three areas decorated like a post office (a mailbox, letter sorter bins, stamps, etc.), a firehouse (fire boots, ladders, pole), and a police station (handcuffs, toy guns, badges, phones, jail cell).

Activities
- Carpool to a real post office, police station, and fire station. Stay long enough for children to see uniforms and have a look around.
- Have children play in your make-believe post office, police station, and fire station.

23

Ragdoll's Delight

Invitations
- Use a ragdoll motif in cloth with yarn for hair and a button for a nose. Draw in the rest of the face.
- Ask children to dress like their favorite ragdoll and to bring their favorite doll to the party.

Activities
- Ragdoll's Ragtime Romp: Have circles of colored tape on the floor (or footprints). Ask children to follow circles or footprints as you play music. When the music stops, the children should be standing inside the circle. If not, they are out of the game. Remove one circle or footprint each time (similar to musical chairs). Provide prizes for all the children who participate.
- Give each child a bag of goodies to take home (have a second bag for their ragdoll).
- Make ragdolls out of yarn and old fabric scraps.

First Formal

For ages 8-12.

Invitations
Invitation should resemble that of a wedding. Formally write out proper names and addresses (even write out number of address).

Decorations
Decorate party area with real or artificial flowers, tall candles, white tablecloths on tables, and formally dressed dolls.

Activities
- Pick up the children with a chauffeur service (can get parents to volunteer). Upon each arrival, have someone announce the name of the guest and blow a horn.
- Have a large box of dress-up clothes including costume jewelry and high heels.
- When everyone is dressed, play music and have the children dance. Videotape if possible.
- Have a special throne for the birthday child to sit in as he or she opens the presents.

Menu
Serve food on trays to children as they "mingle."

25

Crazy Cooks Party

For ages 7-12.

Invitations
Write party information on a paper chef's hat, apron, or menu.

Decorations
Decorate party area with a kitchen theme. Tie the balloons to pots and pans, fill a mixing bowl with popcorn, and have the birthday child wear an apron and chef's hat.

Activities
- Provide cloth aprons as favors and let children decorate their own with fabric paint.
- The main activity is cooking, so let your little chefs go to work. Set up a work station where they can make simple things. A few suggestions might be: make and decorate sandwiches, make fruit sticks, and decorate cupcakes. Ask the birthday child to help plan the menu.

26

Olympic Games Party

Invitations
Create Olympic medals with yarn, foil, and cardboard circles.
Write party information on reverse and child's name on front.

Activities
Think of fun activities that every child can have a chance to win. For example:
- Team activities work well such as a relay race with four members (hop on one foot, walk backwards, crawl, and skip).
- Have an obstacle course.
- Frisbee toss.
- Marble Roll: Roll marbles toward an object and see who comes closest.
- Pie-eating contest.
- Be creative and tailor events to match the children's skills and interests.
- Have an Olympic ceremony at the end before opening presents.

27

Mommy and Daddy Party

The birthday child should call friends at different times of the day and ask what their parents are wearing. For example, before bed or work, during exercise class, or when cleaning the house. The child must come dressed exactly as their parent is at the time of call. You may also send an invitation and tell child what time of day to dress as. Upon arrival, take Polaroid photographs of each child.

Activities
- Make paper picture frames for Polaroid photos. Have the child write a story about their parent on the back.
- Have a parade around the neighborhood.
- Have a parent performance with the children acting like their parents.
- Videotape if possible and play back for the parents when they pick up.

28

December Birthday

I'm Stuck!

Invitations
Make a snowman stuffed with tissue paper. The party information is folded up in snowman's head.

Decorations
Create Santa's house at the North Pole. Gift wrap empty boxes and wrap red and white crepe paper around chairs, pillars, stairs, etc. to look like candy canes. Make reindeer antlers with paper, and felt Santa caps.

Activities
• Make different types of cookies and edible ornaments. You may want to ask a few mothers to help you.
• Organize an elf treasure hunt to find lost toys. Have clues for each destination.
• Open presents at end of party.

29

Follow the Yellow Brick Road

Decorations
Tape a long piece of butcher paper to the floor. Outline bricks with paint or a marker. Collect a broom, witch's hat, a bucket of water, shoes, and a dress. Pile items on floor to represent the Wicked Witch. Ask another adult to dress as Glenda the Good Witch. Hang paper rainbows and flowers on walls to represent Munchkinland.

Activities
- Make Munchkin flower masks by cutting a large ring out of cardboard large enough for child's face to fit in center. Attach flower petals to outside diameter.
- Read *The Wizard of Oz* or play the movie on videotape. Ask children to act out parts. When Dorothy visits Oz, lead the children to a closet where another adult will pretend to be Oz. Have the birthday child hand out party favors.

Menu
Serve rainbow punch using ice cubes made out of different colored juice.

Birthday Express

Invitations
• Make an invitation that resembles a train. Inside, have a pretend ticket for a train trip.

Activities
• Meet at a local train station. Bring cake and presents on train and take a round-trip. Call the station ahead of time to see if your party can visit the engine room.
• Play Gossip: The first child whispers a secret to another. The second child passes on the information until it is heard by all the children. When the information has reached the last child, he or she should say it out loud and see if it is the same as the original.
• Pass the Present: You will need to wrap a prize with several layers of paper. The children pass the gift around while tearing off one layer each. The child who uncovers the last layer gets to keep the prize.

31

Beauty Salon

Create a beauty salon for your child! Collect plenty of old makeup, jewelry, wigs, curlers, brushes, nail polish, etc. Put girls in front of a mirror and help them with their makeup. Have different categories such as most glamorous, silliest, funniest, and new wave. Be sure to have face cream so children can wash off the makeup afterwards.

Invitations
Buy flat makeup sponges and attach party information to them.

Decorations
Decorate house with fashion pictures from magazines.

32

Backwards Party

Invitations
- Write party information backwards.
- Ask guests to dress backwards and unmatched!

Decorations
Tape balloons to the floor and put streamers under the table.

Activities
- Open presents first then sing "Happy Birthday" and eat cake. Eat the meal last!
- Play "Simon Says": Have everyone do the opposite of what you say.
- Set up an obstacle course and start the race from the finish line. Walk the course backwards.

33

Adventure Party

This is an outdoor party, so make sure the children are dressed appropriately.

Decorations
Hang pictures of jungles, deserts, and other adventure destinations.

Activities
- Adventure Tales: Prepare several beginnings to adventure stories, for example, "Walking quietly through the jungle, I heard a loud scream, and turned to see..." Have each child finish the story. This is a good activity to do while waiting for all the guests to arrive.
- Mission Impossible: Have two teams and give each team's leader a map to the first clue. At each location there should be another map leading to the next place. The team that arrives at the final location first wins.

34

Jack and the Beanstalk

For ages 7-12.

Invitations
• Send a card with a picture of a cow on the front and real beans inside.
• Invite the children to come and help Jack climb the beanstalk and get the treasure.

Activities
• When the children arrive, give them a treasure map that will lead them to the first
  clue in finding the giant's castle. Make the following clues hard to find so the children
  work as a team. When they finally find the castle, have a foil-covered treasure box
  with something for each child. Make a large giant on butcher paper and a paper vine
  nearby. Play a tape of "fee fi fo fum" when they approach giant.
• After eating the meal, have a pillow fight to celebrate finding the treasure box.

Menu
Serve a huge submarine sandwich, giant cookies, and lemonade.

35

Let's Go Fly a Kite

Invitations
- Make an invitation that resembles a kite.
- Have the children meet at a park or open area that is good for flying kites.

Activities
- You supply the kites as party favors.
- If the children tire of kite flying, play blindman's bluff. One player is blindfolded, spun around three times, and tries to touch another child. When someone is touched, it is their turn to put the blindfold on.
- Wheelbarrow Races: Form teams of two and have one person walk on their hands while the other holds their feet.
- Serve cake and open presents.

Menu
Pack picnic lunches with all types of goodies.

36

Home on the Range

For boys ages 9 and older.

Invitations
Ask guests to come dressed as cowboys or Indians.

Decorations
Have the party outside in yard or at a park. Start a large campfire to cook food.

Activities
- Catch the Flag: Everyone puts a piece of fabric in their pocket. The idea is to get as many flags as possible. Tackling and tripping are not allowed.
- Play cowboys and Indians. Use squirt guns for a shoot-out.
- Tell stories around the campfire.
- When it is time to open presents, play gift guess. The child holds up a present and the giver gives everyone three clues so they can guess what is inside.

37

Surprise, Surprise

This is a surprise party for the guests as well as the birthday person! Arrange the party for a weekend evening and tell all the kids' parents about the party, but not the children. The real party is a sleepover, so the parents will need to bring a sleeping bag over in advance. Ask parents to have their children in their pajamas at a certain time. The host drives to all the children's houses and picks them up. When they arrive at the house, knock on the door and yell "surprise!"

Activities
- Flashlight Tag: This is similar to regular tag but you shine a light on the others instead of tapping them. This can be played inside or outside.
- Have makeup available for the girls to use on each other.
- Tell ghost stories.

38

Come and Camp

For ages 4-7.

All kids love the outdoors and making forts and tents. This party can also be done inside; it just takes more creativity. Set up one tent for food and another for the presents. If possible, have a campfire and serve camp food including marshmallows for roasting.

Activities
- Make forts! Supply children with plenty of blankets, boxes, large pieces of wood, etc. Organize teams for building forts.
- Have a nature walk and collect twigs, flowers, and leaves. Give each child a lump of clay to stick their finds in. This makes a great centerpiece to take home!

39

In Our Pretty Bonnets

Have a hat decorating party. Buy or have guests bring inexpensive straw hats. Supply ribbons, artificial flowers, paint, glitter, etc. Let the children go outside and gather leaves, twigs, and flowers to add to their creation. After the hats are completed, have a parade and march around the house or neighborhood to show them off. If you have extra time, decorate Easter eggs.

Menu

Provide ingredients for make-your-own sandwiches. Supply different cookie cutters to cut bread, sandwich meats, and cheese. Little girls like to pour their own drinks, so supply a small pitcher and let them pretend they are having a tea party.

40

Hobo Hike

For ages 7-12.

Invitations
• Use red-and-white checkered material and glue to a piece of cardboard.
• Write party information on it with a permanent marker.
• Ask guests to wear old clothes.

Activities
Send the guests into the woods to find long sticks for carrying their
bandana-wrapped lunches. When everyone is ready, choose a leader.
The leader flips a coin to indicate the direction of travel; heads go right
and tails go left. The rest of the line has to follow the leader's steps:
hopping, running, walking, etc. Switch leaders throughout the hike.

Menu
Serve a picnic-style lunch. Have a cooler filled with drinks.

41

Peter Pan Party

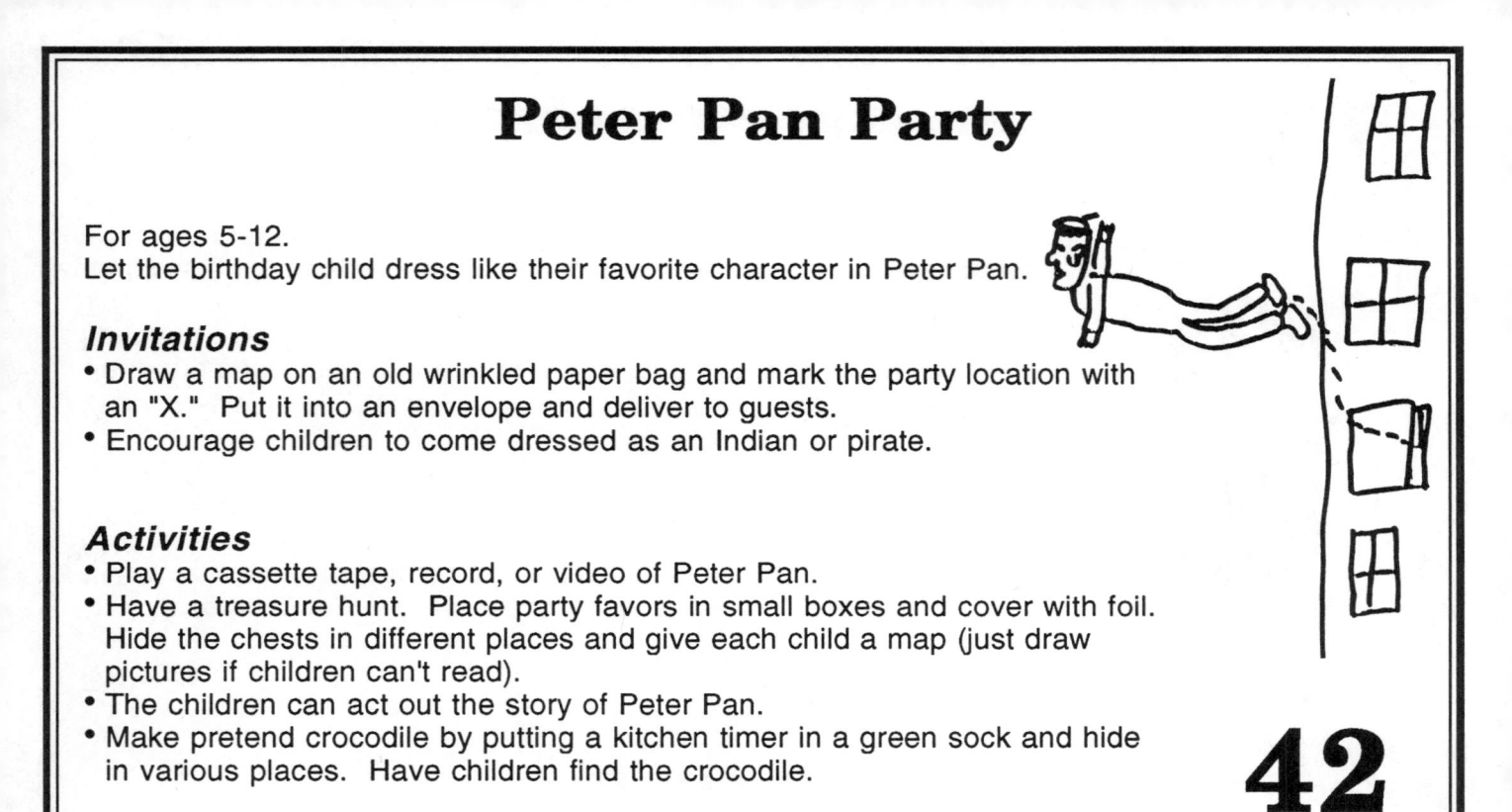

For ages 5-12.
Let the birthday child dress like their favorite character in Peter Pan.

Invitations
- Draw a map on an old wrinkled paper bag and mark the party location with an "X." Put it into an envelope and deliver to guests.
- Encourage children to come dressed as an Indian or pirate.

Activities
- Play a cassette tape, record, or video of Peter Pan.
- Have a treasure hunt. Place party favors in small boxes and cover with foil. Hide the chests in different places and give each child a map (just draw pictures if children can't read).
- The children can act out the story of Peter Pan.
- Make pretend crocodile by putting a kitchen timer in a green sock and hide in various places. Have children find the crocodile.

42

Princess Party

Haven't we all dreamed of being a princess! Have a few mothers come and help be the servants, king, horses, etc. Have various dresses or pieces of fabric available for children to wear as gowns.

Invitations
Send fairy dust and two or three dried peas with invitation. Write the story of the princess and the pea, telling the child to place the peas under her mattress the night before (to make sure that they are real princesses).

Activities
• Make crowns out of cardboard cones with glitter, crepe paper, etc. Attach a long flowing piece of fabric to tip.
• Make an enchanted web with yarn. Have each child's yarn be a different color and run the web around the entire room and furniture.
• A prize could be tied to the end of the yarn.

Menu
Serve hot chocolate in tea cups with petit cakes. Have princesses sit on pillows while they eat.

43

Birthday Bug Bash

Invitations
Cut out large ladybugs, caterpillars, spiders, etc. from a coloring book. Use these as a pattern for making invitations. They should be colorful and have yarn and other items glued on.

Activities
- What Bug am I?: Have a child whisper to adult what bug they are going to act out. The other children guess the answer and the winner goes next.
- Bug Treasure Hunt: Give each team of two a safe, plastic bug jar (puncture small holes in lid). Set a time limit. The team with the most bugs wins the game.
- Swatter's Tag: Form two teams and make homemade fly swatters with popsicle sticks and soft netting. Once an opposing team member is swatted, they are out of the game. The team with the most players left at the end is the winner.
- Make party hats with plastic spiders, bugs, and butterflies glued to outside.

Menu
Serve a simple picnic lunch outside consisting of hot dogs, vegetable tray, watermelon, baked beans, chips, punch, and a ladybug-shaped cake.

Sports Party

Invitations
Deliver a plastic ball for whatever sport you will be highlighting. Write party information on outside.

Decorations
Decorate party area according to the sport the children will be playing. Use posters, pictures from sports magazines, etc.

Activities
• Play sports trivia.
• Have a parent be an announcer and interview each player. Videotape interviews and play videotape while everyone eats ice cream and cake.
• The birthday person has to answer easy sports questions correctly before opening each present (guests can help).

Menu
Serve ballpark food such as hot dogs, popcorn, cola, cake, and ice cream.

45

My Name is Bozo

Invitations
- Invitation should have a clown picture on the cover.
- Ask guests to come dressed as clowns.

Decorations
Hang balloons of all shapes and colors around the party area. Put clown posters on the walls.

Activities
- Hire a clown to juggle and perform magic tricks.
- Play "Pin the Pom-Pom on the Clown."
- Kids could get together in groups of 2-4 and make up circus acts.

Activities Option
- Take children to circus performance.
- Paint children's faces upon arrival.

Menu
Serve a clown-shaped cake with ice cream and punch.

46

Doctor, Doctor, Nurse, Nurse

For ages 7-12.

Invitations
• Use a medical theme and tape a band-aid to the front of invitation.
• Ask guests to come dressed as a doctor, dentist, or nurse.

Decorations
Decorate party area to resemble a doctor's office or hospital area. Put white sheets on tabletops and have paper hospital gowns and plastic gloves available.

Activities
• Ask a Red Cross instructor to come and teach the children first aid.
• Have a skit called "Emergency, Emergency...Help Please": Divide into groups and give each group 10-15 minutes to rehearse a skit. Pre-write an easy and humorous drama for them to follow, using skills taught by the first aid instructor. The children will present the skits to each other.

47

Animal House Party

Invitations
- Cut out different animal shapes and write party information on front.
- Each guest should dress in costume of a favorite animal.

Decorations
Put green crepe paper and posters of tropical trees and animals on walls to create a "jungle" effect.

Activities
- Guess identity of each guest as they arrive.
- Have an animal parade and offer a prize for the best animal characterization.
- Play music and have dances such as the "bunny hop," "tiger rag," "elephant walk," etc.

Menu
Serve a simple meal of hamburgers, hot dogs, cola, cookies, nuts, bananas, and trail mix.

48

Fast Food Round Robin

Invitations
- Collect place mats or unused food containers from restaurants included in round robin. Write party information on paper and glue or staple to place mat/food container.
- Pre-plan food orders by enclosing an order form with invitation asking each guest what he/she wants to eat.
- Ask parents to volunteer to serve as drivers. Decorate cars and provide maps with routes to each stop.

Menu
Plan meal to begin at one restaurant for an appetizer, perhaps a salad at Wendy's. The party continues to McDonalds for sandwiches and French fries. Then have dessert at an ice cream shop. Call restaurant managers ahead to reserve seating and for party favors which are often available.

Activities
Follow the meal with a game of miniature golf or bowling, or play games at a nearby park.

49

Bicycle Photo Safari

Ages 9-13 years.
This party is a treasure hunt on bicycles.

Invitations
- Use a bicycle or camera motif for invitation.
- Ask guests to bring their bicycles.

Activities
- You will need to purchase a disposable camera for each guest, or team of 2-3 guests.
- Plan a tour of your neighborhood and photo locations and create a simple "safari clues list." Your guests must use the clue list and photograph the location they believe is correct within a determined time limit.
- Make arrangements with a one-hour photo store to have the film processed while guests are eating dinner.
- Display photographs on a large wall. Photographs of correct locations will be judged for artistic quality, and prizes will be awarded.

Menu
Pizza, dips, potato chips, finger fruit, Jello, and a cake that resembles a camera.

Kidnap Breakfast Surprise

Ages 13-17.
This is a popular theme for a birthday or a celebration
for an accomplishment.

Invitations
- Arrange to "kidnap" guest of honor in early
  morning hours before school.
- Ask guests to wear pajamas.
- It is best to invite guests personally or by telephone.
  Make sure they know this is a surprise.

Decorations
Bring a bouquet of balloons for the guest of honor.

Menu
Make reservations at a local restaurant serving breakfast. It can be very
amusing to go to a restaurant wearing your pajamas!

51

Right to Vote

This party is best for an eighteenth birthday party.

Invitations
Use a campaign theme. Include with party information a button with photo of guest of honor on it for everyone to wear.

Decorations
Hang balloons, streamers, campaign posters, and straw hats with ribbons.

Activities
• Have guests submit campaign slogans for the guest of honor. Offer a prize for the best one.
• Guest of honor should give an acceptance speech on becoming eighteen years old.
• Guests should each write a humorous story about birthday person and place in a secret ballot box. A "speaker of the house" will read stories aloud and guests will vote on the best one.

Menu
Sandwich buffet with a birthday cake in the shape of "18."

52

Round 'em Up, Head 'em Out

Invitations
- Create a wanted poster by placing a picture of guest of honor on front. Burn edges for antique look.
- Arrange for teens to meet at farm, park, or trail ride facility.
- Guests should wear jeans.

Decorations
Use an old western town motif by hanging "wanted posters," posters from rodeos, and pictures of horses. Place a red-and-white checkered tablecloth on tables.

Activities
Go on a trail ride. Horses should be reserved in advance according to riders' experience levels. Party size may have to be limited, so check in advance. Rides usually range from one to two hours.

Menu
Bring long sub-sandwich from a local deli, chips, dip, sodas, and juice.

53

Softball All-Stars Party

Hold party at local park. Reserve baseball field for games.

Invitations
Cut lightweight cardboard into shape of a baseball. Fold at top and print party information inside.
Ask guests to bring baseball mitts.

Decorations
Use mitts and balls for table centerpieces.

Menu
Serve hot dogs with potato chips, popcorn, and peanuts. Ice cream sundaes
for dessert.

Games
Select teams and play a softball game.

54

Career Party

Age 16 and up.

This is not a celebration party, rather a self-discovery party. Teens are all searching for what they want to be. Arrange for friends in varied professions ranging from doctor, construction worker, beautician, professional athlete, stewardess, etc. Get as many as you can, possibly using the parents of the guests. Give the career parents big name tags on which to write their profession. The object of the party is for teens to be able to talk to adults in an informal setting about what they do.

Menu
Finger food, lemonade, fruit, and vegetables with dip.

55

Future Shock Year 3000

Invitations

Fold blank piece of paper in half. Write on front "In the Future...." Inside write information about party. Ask guests to come dressed as part of their future.

Menu

Serve frozen T.V. dinners and Tang.

Activities

- Future Predictions: Everyone writes as many predictions as they would like. Fold up and place in hat. Pass around circle. Each person reads a few.
- Divide into teams and make up a future dance.
- 20 Questions: Each person stands up and according to what they are wearing the rest of the group tries to guess their future. They have 20 questions, and person answers them yes or no.

56

Packing Up and Camping Out

Invitations
- Reserve a camping site in advance.
- Use a camping tent motif with information attached inside. Ask for an R.S.V.P. Include information for parents such as where you can be reached while camping and a map.
- Enlist parents to assist, and assign tents, bedrolls, and other equipment.

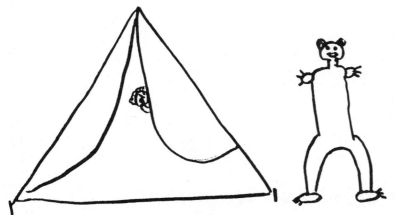

Menu
Hot dogs, soup, s'mores, doughnuts, and hot chocolate.

Activities
Treasure hunts, trail walks, campfire stories, and singing (if possible, bring a guitar).

57

Powder Puff Party

Hold party at local park or school football field. Provide footballs, referee striped shirts, whistles, pads, and helmets to boys to bring for girls.

Invitations
Use small football shapes. Information inside. Ask boys and girls to wear very casual sports clothes.

Menu
Picnic of deli foods, brownies, fruit, and lots of Gatorade.

Activities
Girls pick teams (draw numbers). Boys are picked for coaches, trainers, equipment managers, cheerleaders. Girls to bring pom-poms for boys. Football game played as long as desired.

Awards
Trophies (handmade): most valuable player, most tackles, most points, etc.

58

Pancake Project Breakfast

Encourage your teens! Hold this party before a scheduled teen "project," i.e., car wash, raffle sales, yard cleaning, walk-, bike-, skate-, or jog-a-thon.

Invitations
- Cut out spatula and pancake shapes from construction paper. Write party information on back.
- Ask guests to bring their favorite ingredient for pancakes (blueberries, strawberries, chocolate chips, etc.).

Decorations
- Plastic pancake spatulas with ribbons with guests' names on them tied to handles.
- Pancake mix boxes with flowers as centerpieces.

Activities
Let guests flip pancakes, add favorite ingredients, and eat! eat! eat! Favorite CD's playing in background. After breakfast, teens head for project full of energy and pancakes!

59

PGA Miniature Golf Party

This is a great outing party which requires some advance planning. Make reservations at a miniature putting course. Pick up score cards and attach to invitation.

Invitations
Have guests meet at putting course and include a map with directions.

Activities
Guests can play for prizes as individual competitors or as teams.

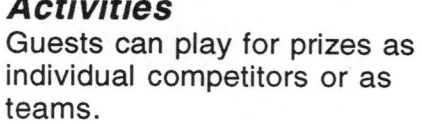

Menu
If course has a snack bar, let guests choose what they want to eat. If not, bring sandwiches, drinks, and cake.

60

Pizza Party with a Twist

Invitations
- Cut out a pizza shape and draw pepperonis on front. Write party information on reverse.
- Guests should wear very casual clothes.

Activities
- Play "Twister" (may be purchased at a toy store): Have guests divide into teams to play.
- Play fifties style background music.

Menu
Pizza, of course! Have it delivered or make it at home. Serve with soda, juices, brownies, and ice cream.

61

Couples Crazy Valentine Party

Invitations

Send to girls only. Girls ask boys to party.
Write on invitation, "Roses are red, violets are blue, I am crazy and so are you." Ask guests to write stories of their "craziest" date or party experience, to share.

Activities

• Upon entering the party, give each guest an eyebrow pencil to decorate their date's face in a funny way (for example, glasses, a mustache, chicken pox, freckles, etc.).
• Dance Contest: Divide into partners and tie right wrists together. Couples have 15 minutes to make up a dance together. Do dance one couple at a time. Group votes on winner.
• Pie-Eating Contest: Buy small frozen pie crusts. Fill with pudding. Awards for fastest eater, neatest, etc.

Menu

Serve red food and a heart-shaped cake.

62

Detective Party

Ages 15 and older.

Invitations and Activities
- There are many detective games available from toy and game stores that include invitations, give you clues and set-up for the detective plot. All you have to do is play the game.
- Request that guests dress as the character they will be playing in the mystery story. Send character descriptions from game box with the invitations to prepare your guests for an exciting party.
- However, if you feel extra creative, you can write your own mystery plot and hide the clues around the party area before guests arrive.
- Allow guests time to question each other's characters, search for clues, and solve the detective story. Collect all guests together and decide who is guilty.
- Serve refreshments while solving mystery.

63

Soap Opera Surprise

This is a perfect party for a sorority house, dorm, high school, or anyone who follows the soaps! Plan the party to take place while your show is on the air, or videotape the show and play it during an evening party.

Decorations
Cut out pictures of soap opera characters from a fan magazine and paste your guest of honor's picture on the faces of the stars.

Activities
After the soap opera is over, try acting out a story based on the guest of honor's life. The best idea would be for the hostess to write a script and have the guests act it out.

64

Dance Party

Ages 10 and older.

Invitations
Make a record or use an old 45. Write party information in the center.

Activities
- Hire someone to teach a new dance to guests.
- Make up dance games. For example, when the music stops, everyone must freeze, and those who move must step out of the game.
- Dance Train: Hold on to each other and dance around the room.
- Dance Contest: Award prizes for fastest, funniest, and most original.
- Follow the Leader: Everyone must do the same dance as the leader. Start with the birthday person.

Menu
Serve make-your-own pizza with English muffins, spaghetti sauce, etc.
Follow with a make-your-own sundae.

65

Star Search

Girls ages 12 and older.

Decorations
Set up a stage area where guests can perform.
Videotape the acts if possible.

Invitations
- Decorate huge stars with glitter and a picture of a model or movie star in center.
- Tell guests to come prepared with an act to be performed alone or with a group.

Activities
- Each guest performs an act.
- Promotional Contest: You will need a tray of items such as make up, hairspray, clothing, etc. Individually, the guests must stand and endorse a product. The audience must clap for the best performances, and a prize is given to the winner.

66

Pajama Party

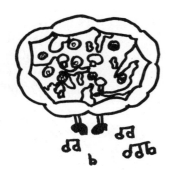

Girls ages 12 and older.

Invitations
Begin the party after dinner. Make sure to invite a manageable number of girls (between four and six children).

Menu
An organized "raid the refrigerator" in which the guest can choose and make what they would like. Pre-stock the refrigerator with food that you know they will enjoy.

Activities
• Have a scavenger hunt around the house.
• Take turns reading ghost stories aloud.

67

Me and My Mime Party

This is a teen party that is best for those who have had some acting or miming experience.

Invitations
Use a white mime face and write information in black ink on reverse.

Decorations
Set up a stage area, with director chairs, spotlights, etc.

Activities
- Have a professional mime give a presentation and teach technique, gestures, positions, etc.
- Divide into teams and act out different scenes (like charades). Actors' team must guess in a 2-3 minute time period to win points for their team.

68

A Day in Court

This is a teen birthday party particularly for one who is an aspiring police officer, judge, or lawyer.

- Try to find a judge who will allow your group to visit his or her courtroom and chambers.
- Most public buildings have a social room or a cafeteria where you can hold your "birthday party," or you can stop at a restaurant after the day in court.

Activities
- Arrange for guests to take turns sitting on judge's bench while wearing a black robe. Videotape this if possible.
- Divide into teams and hold mock trials. Allow 10-15 minutes for each team to plan the case. Let the "party jury" decide the outcome of each trial.

69

Marathon Birthday Party

This is a great party for a running enthusiast.

Invitations
- Use the map of a marathon course that will be run.
- Name the marathon after the birthday person.
- Ask for R.S.V.P.
- Dress should be running or workout attire.

Activities
You will need three to five helpers to stay at beverage spots along the route. The finish will be at party area. Hang a finish line (ribbon) and present award medals to the runners (perhaps you can have T-shirts printed commemorating the party). The party can be held at a home or a park, but should have a barbeque area.

Menu
Vegetable tray, barbequed chicken, and carrot cake.

70

Bean Party

Invitations
"Bean porridge hot, bean porridge cold,
Bean porridge in the pot nine days old.
Join us as we honor (name)
at (place, date, and time).
Bring as your gift, one gift-wrapped can of any type of beans."

Decorations
Decorate party area with green crepe paper (or real) vines.

Activities
- Bean Guessing: Fill a jar with jelly beans and have guests guess how many are there. The winner receives the jelly beans.
- Bean Toss: Use a large board with different sized holes. Throw bean bags through the holes. The smaller holes are worth more points; the larger holes are worth one point.

Menu
Serve bean soup, cornbread, beverages, and a bean-shaped cake.

71

Surprise Birthday for Me

Turn the tables! Invite close friends to a party at your place.

Activities
- When everyone has arrived, announce "happy birthday to me" and send yourself a singing birthday gram! The surprise is on your guests.
- Ask the guests to make you a birthday gift in a 30-minute time limit. Provide arts and crafts materials and set a timer. Offer a prize for the best "creation" and allow the guests to vote.

Menu
Have a table laden with a tasty selection of hot and cold dishes, desserts, and beverages.

72

Women's Bridge Party

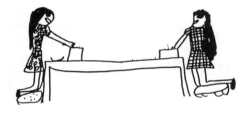

Instead of guests bringing their favorite recipe, have them bring their best menu for a fantastic dinner. They should bring enough copies for the others and include notes on how to make the meal successful.

Activities
- Have a napkin folding demonstration. If you don't know different folding techniques, hire a professional. Have plenty of napkins to go around so everyone can practice and take their creations home as party favors.
- Play bridge.

Menu
Serve finger foods and beverages.

73

On the Spot Party

Have you ever visited a friend or relative without knowing that it is their birthday or anniversary? There is no need to fret. The following "on the spot parties" call for an "on the spot" guest list.

Invitations
• Usually, there is only time for telephoning the guests. Enlist friends to assist you with the calls.
• Let the guest of honor know about the party and have input on guests.

Decorations
You will need balloons, streamers, hats, signs, etc. You can decorate after guests arrive.

Activities
• Cut out ads from a newspaper of items that you and your guests will buy for the guest of honor. Have guests put their clipping in an envelope which they might decorate before presenting it.
• Hide items around the house and give points to the person who finds the most.

Menu
The cake is also a last-minute creation. Use cake mix and ready-made frosting. Guests help bake and clean up.

74

Hello to Hollywood

Invitations
- Create black-and-white movie call boards and write party information on reverse.
- Ask guests to come in costume as their favorite movie star. They should portray the character throughout the party including mannerisms, gestures, and speech.
- Greet guests with a video camera and have "fans" ask for autographs.
- Enlist help of teenage friends for "fans."

Decorations
Decorate party room like a movie set. Call a local school's drama department to borrow props. Use glitter and glitz, by using foil, sequined material, tinsel, etc. Use plenty of lighting as spotlights.

Activities
- Have a costume contest and provide prizes such as movie passes.
- Silver Screen Trivia: Choose teams and ask each other trivia questions.

75

Husband's Reign Stag Party

Invitations
- Make invitation in the shape of saws, hammers, and other tools. You can even cut and paste pictures of tools found in catalogues and magazines.
- Gift suggestions might be tools and yard care equipment.
- Party can be a surprise for guest of honor.

Decorations
Hang pictures of tools on walls and from ceilings. Borrow a large stand-up poster from hardware store and glue a photograph of guest of honor's head on it and place in party area.

Activities
- Best "hardware or tool" joke contest. Prize for winner selected by party guests.
- "I Can Build This in Five Minutes!": Buy simple wood project kits from hardware or hobby shops. Contest is to see who can build the kit in the best time according to the kit's instructions.

Menu
Serve a hearty meal with plenty of beverages. Have a birthday cake in the shape of a tool.

76

Fabulous Forties Birthday Party

Invitations
- Send your invitation in the form of a 45 rpm record or buy used records and glue information to center.
- Guests should wear forties clothes.

Decorations
Hang posters around the room of famous forties stars (Joan Crawford, Spencer Tracy, Katharine Hepburn, Orson Welles), World War II, and war bonds.

Activities
- Have a jitterbug contest and award ribbons to winners based on enthusiasm, style, and endurance.
- Play the oldies such as Benny Goodman, Glenn Miller, and Frank Sinatra.

Menu
Serve hamburgers, French fries, cola, cupcakes, and twinkies.

77

I Lost Track of Time

This theme is good when you cannot celebrate the birthday on the right day, or if it was temporarily forgotten.

Invitations
• Copy the face of "Big Ben" clock. Make a hole in the middle and fasten a brass tack. Attach cardboard hands that will spin around.
• Request guests to wear their clothing and/or costumes backwards.

Activities
• Guests tell stories of times dates were forgotten or they showed up late for an event. Tell the story backwards!
• Choose teams and give each a large spoon and a potato. The first team to carry the potato over a finish line (walking backwards) and drop it in a bag is the winner. Each member must carry it back and forth once and pass it on to the next person.

Menu
Serve the dessert first, and follow with the main course, salad, appetizers, and beverages.

78

Man of the Year

Invitations
- Have the father's picture put on a mock magazine cover. Make several copies and have the headline read, "Man of the Year."
- Male guests should wear tuxedos or suits and ties. Women should wear dresses.

Decorations
Collect photos of father and make a collage for displaying at party.

Menu
- Serve father's favorite meal.
- Guests should each make a champagne toast after dinner.

79

Surprise Workout Party

This party is for the busy career person who only has time for working out.

Invitations
Use a bodybuilder theme. Pre-arrange with birthday person's health club to have party there. Guests should come dressed in their workout clothes.

Decorations
Decorate in advance. Hang a poster of a bodybuilder and paste a photo of the birthday person's face on it.

Activities
• Wait until the birthday person works up a sweat in the exercise room before surprising him or her.
• Play music and dance after the meal.

Menu
Serve beer, pizza, and cake.

80

Top of Parking Lot Party

Invitations
Use parking lot ticket with information about party.

Activities
• Rent top level of parking lot in city. View of city lights a must!
• Band or D.J. for dancing the night away under the stars.

Menu
Rent food wagon vendors with hot dogs, hot pretzels, popcorn, tacos, ice cream, etc.
Or, set up stations and hire teenagers to staff.

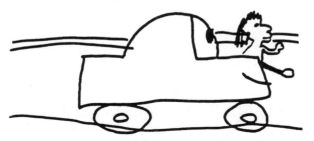

81

Surprise Slumber Party

 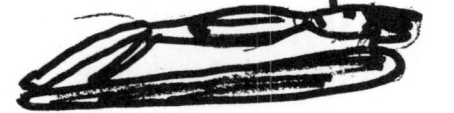

This party is for women only. Everyone will remember their high school days!

Have a surprise slumber party for your wife or girlfriend's 50th birthday. Have the party a few days in advance so she won't expect it. Invite friends to come over late in the evening, wear their pajamas, and bring their sleeping bags and favorite records.

Menu
- Serve chilled champagne, fresh chocolate-tipped strawberries, and canapés.
- Serve a light breakfast in the morning.

82

Let's Flip Our Wigs

Contact a wig store and arrange to have a wig show and demonstration with all types and colors for guests to try. Arrange to have a cosmetic salesperson to do makeovers and consultations. Play background music.

Activities
- Photograph the makeovers and let the guests take the photographs home as party favors.
- Present birthday girl with a wig of her choice, a day at the beauty salon, and massage certificates.

Menu
Serve a light luncheon buffet with fruit punch and cake.

83

Mixing Business with Pleasure

This is a party to show clients or friends a new office or warehouse.
Hire a local school bus or van to pick up guests at host's home.
The guests should not know where the party is being held.

Invitations
- Make invitation in the shape of a question mark and write party information on it.
- It might be fun to plan stops along the way to the party, such as a fast food restaurant, a golf course, park, miniature golf, etc.

Activities
- Have a song leader and musician on the bus to entertain while enroute to party.
- Have the party catered and hire some form of music, which should be in full swing when guests arrive at your new place of business.

84

Tailgate Birthday Celebration

This party is great for the sports nut. What would be a better way to honor their birthday than treating them and their friends to a tailgate party before or after a football, soccer, baseball, softball, or hockey game?

Invitations
Print party information on a copy of an old program of the sport you will be attending.

Activities
• Play a sports trivia game while waiting for the game to begin.
• Gifts may be sports items, tickets to sporting events, etc.

Menu
• Have a barbeque in parking lot before game begins.
• Guests should bring their lounge chairs, grills, coolers, etc.

85

King for a Night

Hire a limousine and arrange a date (may be wife or girlfriend) for your "King for the Night" (the limousine should be stocked with beverages). The limousine drives the "King" to different spots around town where friends can be seen holding posters and signs with funny quotes on them which relate to the "King." Once the limo has passed each guest's spot, everyone goes to the party and waits for the "King" to arrive. Finally, the limo will arrive at the host's house for a surprise party.

Invitations
• Purchase gold crowns and print party information on the inside.
• Ask each couple to wait at assigned locations with a large poster with a funny quote intended to be seen by the birthday "King."

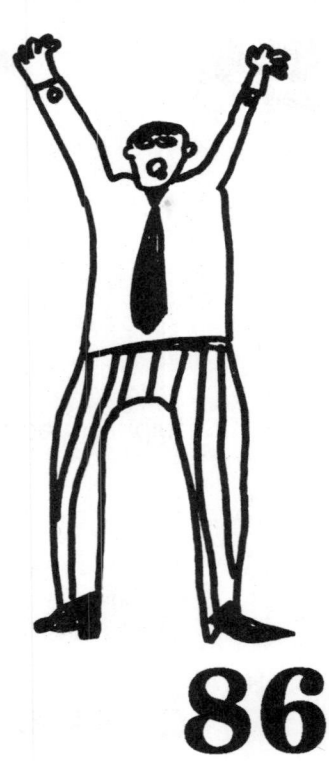

86

Bocce Ball Birthday

This is a great summertime party with an Italian theme.

Invitations
- The invitations should resemble the Italian flag with party information on the back.
- Ask guests to wear red, white, or green.

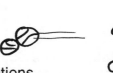

Activities
- Set up a bocce ball (lawn bowling) area. Have rules and regulations available for guests to read. Play a round robin tournament and assign someone to referee the games.
- Play lively Italian music.

Menu
Serve a buffet of Italian dishes from lasagne to cannoli and wine.

Turn About Birthday

Birthday party for a friend who does not wish to be the guest of honor. Express your desire to celebrate friend's birthday by hosting a party at the charity of their choice (example: Childrens Hospital, Nursing Home, Handicap Center, etc.).

Invitations
- Contact charity chosen by birthday friend and ask if you can host a party for their people.
- Send invitations to friends of birthday person and ask them to bring appropriate gifts to be distributed at party. (Or one large joint gift to the charity.)
- Request R.S.V.P.

Decorations
Balloons, hats, paper streamers, fresh flowers for each guest.

Activities
- Live entertainment by local school or personal friends.
- Sing-a-longs, or a magic show.

Menu
- Serve menu recommended by the facility (as diets may vary).
- Enlist the aid of the facility's kitchen staff in planning menu.

88

Rib Tickler Party

There is a hidden comedian in all of us! This party will give your friends a chance to "star" in their own stand-up comedy act. Or, if you simply want to entertain them, hire a local comedian to perform and give comedy "tips."

Invitations
Create your personalized logo for your own comedy club, i.e., use initials of name or make up name. Invite guests to come with their favorite jokes to share.

Decorations
- Set card tables around party area, leaving area in front or in middle for "stage area."
- Set up spotlight and microphone. Candles or low lights on tables and around the room. Create a nightclub effect.

Menu
Have waitress or waiter to serve drinks and snacks at each table.

89

Fifties Fantasy Sock Hop

Hold party at home or rent local hall or hotel party room.
Will need room for dancing and "fifties" contests.

Invitations

Cut out a picture of a saddle shoe and paste on cardboard.
Invitation to read: Put on your favorite jeans, T-shirts, and letter jackets, or your poodle skirts, bobby socks, and saddle oxford shoes and enjoy the fabulous sounds of the fifties. Sock-hop, games, and contests. Exciting evening of food, fun, and great music. Lots of prizes too!

Activities

Costume Contest - Dance Contest - Hula Hoop Contest - and Bubble Gum Blowing Contest.
The Grand Finale: A lip sync contest.

Decorations

Balloons, streamers, and a fifties stage with screen and music
personalities' pictures.

Menu

Serve sandwiches, fruit, chips, beverages, and a birthday cake.

90

The ABC's of Motherhood

Decorate room with ABC wall hangings and wood blocks. Make a block cake by cutting cake into squares and icing the sides. Ask each guest to bring a present beginning with a designated letter, and a verse written about the necessity of the object brought.

Activities
• Have each person write their ABC's of motherhood (their three most important words of advice or encouragement).
• Place something in the party room that begins with each letter of the alphabet. Have guests write down what they can see in the room from A to Z.

91

Pink and Blue

Decorations
- Everything must be in pink and blue, from food and dress to invitations.
- Divide guests into two teams (pink and blue). The team with the most points by the end of the shower wins.

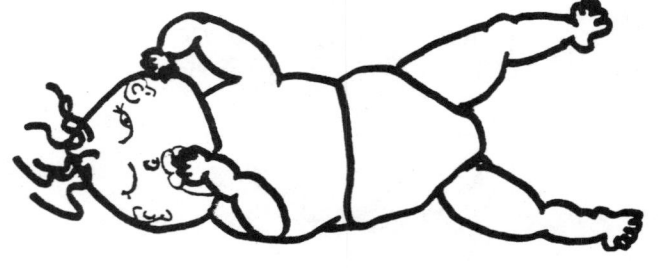

Activities
- Nursery Advertisements: Remove all identifying names from large color advertisements of baby products, then number and post around the room. The guests get one point for each correct answer.
- Price Game: Line up various baby supplies. Have people guess the price. The closest wins ten points per item.
- Bottle Race: Half fill bottles with juice or soda pop and have each team drink from the bottles through a nipple. The first bottle to be empty wins.

92

Sibling Shower

Have this shower a month after the baby is born. Invite other mothers to bring their young children. Play games and have a good time. Focus on the older children. Gifts are brought for the siblings, for being such a great brother or sister. All children should receive a prize. Have all the kids talk about their new brother or sister and what it is like to be older.

93

The Way We Were

This is a shower for couples. The idea is to come dressed as and to act as they did before they had children or, if no children, as they imagine themselves to be with children. Everyone must come with a picture of their wedding.

This is a very casual, fun get-together. Before gifts are opened, each couple shows their wedding pictures and describes how their life has changed since they had children. Try to keep these short and fun.

Menu
Serve wedding cake and champagne.

94

Chosen One

As soon as the adopting family has received word that their chosen one is soon to arrive, it is time to send the invitations. This is a good shower to include the entire family. This gives the family a chance to introduce their child to all their friends. It also gives the child a chance to meet some young friends. Be sure to prepare food that children as well as adults would like. Casual visiting and playing is appropriate.

95

Carpenters' Convention

Invitations
Write information on a piece of paper and glue it to a piece of wood.

Activities
This is a good father shower for men who are handy. Furniture can be built or simply assembled. If furniture is to be built, make sure to have a pattern and supplies. Put some good music on and make sure to have lots of goodies available for the hard workers.

96

Day at the Spa

Gather a group of women friends together and spend a day at a spa. Get facials, massages, mud baths, etc. Have lunch or dinner together. Everyone pays for their own and chips in for the mother-to-be who is treated like a queen. One gift can be purchased by the whole group and given to the mother-to-be. Indulge yourself!

97

Stork Shower

Send invitations with storks on the front. Make or rent a large stork to stand near the front door to collect presents!

Activities

- Feather Blowing Contest: Two teams stand opposite each other. Each team tries in a cooperative effort to blow the feather into the other team's territory. The first team to have the feather touch the floor three times on their side loses the game.
- Stork Bowl: This is played with teams also. Have members of one team stand on one leg like storks (can hop back and forth) but not on two legs at the same time. The other team has three rubber balls. Each player has a chance to roll the balls at the storks. Whenever someone leans against another, touches the floor, etc. one point is given. Switch sides. The team with the most points wins.
- Night Flight: Turn off the lights and give each person a paper and pencil. Close eyes and draw a road, a house, and landscape where stork will land, one at a time.

98

New Mothers Welcome to Neighborhood Party

Invitations

- It is best to call over the phone or invite the guests in person.
- This should be a casual, informal, non-threatening get-together for the new mothers in the neighborhood.
- This can be a brunch or a continental breakfast.
- Invite guests to bring preschoolers along.
- Hire a baby-sitter and have a play area available, so all the mothers can visit.

Activities

- Ice Breaker: "Your best piece of advice to another mother..." and "My most embarrassing moment with my new baby..."
- As each new mother leaves the party, give her cookies or a casserole to take home.

99

Share a Book

Invitations
Write shower information on the back of a pretty bookmark.
Ask all guests to bring the book they felt was most helpful
when they were new mothers.

Activities
When expecting a new baby, all mothers feel overwhelmed
with their lack of knowledge. Most of us don't know which of
the hundreds of child care books to pick up first! As the
mother-to-be unwraps each book, share the reasons the book
was important to you, and make a wish for the new mother.

100

End of Your Personal Life

Invite all the father-to-be's friends to a men's night together.
Keep to the baby theme.

Activities
- Baby Obstacle Course: Divide into teams of three or four. The team to finish the course first wins. Start by diapering (using cloth diapers) a plastic baby doll. Next, crawl two times around the room, undress baby, and place baby in a bucket of water (bath). Run to next teammate and feed him five spoons of applesauce. Each player must do the whole course.
- Baby Food Testing Game: Give evaluation sheet to each guest.

Menu
Serve your favorite beverage in baby bottles (poke extra large holes in nipples) and let men choose favorite jar of baby food.

101

Weight Watching Party

So all of your friends seem to be on a diet? Don't fret - have a party anyway! Serve healthy food so no one has to feel guilty. Have everyone come in workout clothes with good walking shoes. Find a hiking path in your area and meet there for a group hike. Finish the party at your home. Serve healthy refreshments.

Ideas
This would be a fun theme for an aerobics class or this could be a group baby shower for a prenatal class. Have everyone bring one present and exchange them!

102

Career Fair

This is a shower for fathers. They are to come dressed as what they dream their child will become. Make sure guests come prepared to convince the group why the child should want to be what they picked.

Menu
Serve hero sandwiches and dream puffs.

103

Mother Goose

Invitations
- Send an invitation with a Mother Goose rhyme on it replacing some of the words with party information.
- All gifts are to be nursery rhymes and food should be found in rhymes (example, tarts, brown bread and butter sandwiches, strawberries and cream, etc.).

Activities
- Mother Goose Charades: Divide into teams. The player must act out nursery rhyme and team must guess correctly within three minutes to receive a point. The team with the most points wins.
- Verse Memory: Form teams. One team says the first two lines of a nursery rhyme. The opposing team says next two. The team to first say the wrong words scores a point. The team with the most points loses the game! Make sure to have a nursery rhyme book handy to judge.

104

Gifts for Mother

This is an especially nice shower to give a mother who already has one or two children. This should be an elegant evening. The mother is to feel glamorous and special. Decorate the room with candles, play classical music, and have the guests come dressed in formal attire. Serve fine food. The gifts are for the mother, for example, perfume, lingerie, makeup, etc.

105

Nursery "Deco" Party

Invitations

- Write party information on a piece of a rag and add paper confetti to the envelope (as magic cleaning dust!).
- Invite your friends to come and help paint, wallpaper, line drawers, set up changing table, and all other nursery jobs. This is especially helpful if the mother-to-be has been ordered off her feet or doesn't feel well.
- Supply paper hats and aprons.
- Make clear on invitations that the gift is help, and no presents are needed! Serve finger foods since all will be too busy to sit down.

106

What Child is This?

Invitations
- Cut out baby photos and glue to a piece of paper. Make photocopies and fold. Write party information inside.
- Ask guests to bring their own baby photos and four or five items of information on their life "as a baby."
- Gifts: Good ideas might be a diaper service, baby-sitting coupons, dinners, cleaning services, etc.

Activities
- Mount guests' photos on a posterboard. Let guests view them, but don't reveal the identifications. Collect "items of information" on each guest and place in a container. Pass container around and let guests choose one sheet and match it to a photo. Finish game by having the guests claim their photos and tell baby stories about themselves.
- "How Fast Can You Change the Baby?": This can be played by teams, or as a relay. You will need a life-size doll, diapers, pins, and a timer.

107

Pass it On

This shower is for current mothers to give for the mother-to-be. Bring any unused, hard-to-find, or loanable baby items. Tips are one of the most important pass-on items for a new mother, so make sure many are written down. The guests may bring tips or write them down in a book supplied by the hostess.

Menu
Serve dessert, coffee, tea, hot chocolate, and cider.

108

Baby First Aid

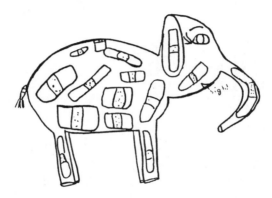

Invitations

• Invite other mothers you know to an afternoon of learning first aid.
• Make sure to contact a Red Cross instructor to come to instruct the class. How much more fun to learn with friends! If there is a fee for the class, let the women know when you call to invite them.

Menu

Have an afternoon tea with small cakes, tarts, and finger sandwiches.

109

Second Chance

Here is your chance to have a shower for a grandmother-to-be. Her house needs to be outfitted and ready to entertain grandchildren! Focus on gifts such as toys, or a group gift of a crib, playpen, or high chair. Let new grandmother talk a little about her grandchild and how different it feels to be a grandmother.

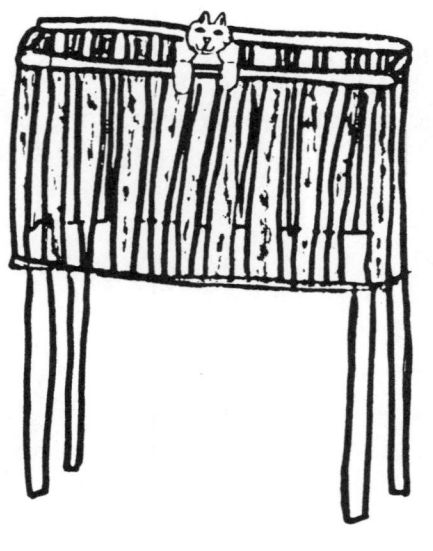

Menu
Serve chicken salad, a luscious dessert, and tea.

110

Learn Baby Massage

We all love to be touched! Invite all the mothers of children under eight months to learn baby massage. You may be able to find an instructor in your area to come and teach the class, or teach it yourself with the aid of a book or *video. Massage is calming and is a very beautiful way to bond with your baby. Use pure vegetable oil, warmed in your hands, and then apply it to baby.

*An excellent video to learn infant massage is **Baby Bonding** which can be ordered by sending $24.95 to: *Forward March™ Video*
831 Sweeney Avenue, Suite G
Redwood City, CA 94063

111

Rock Around the Clock

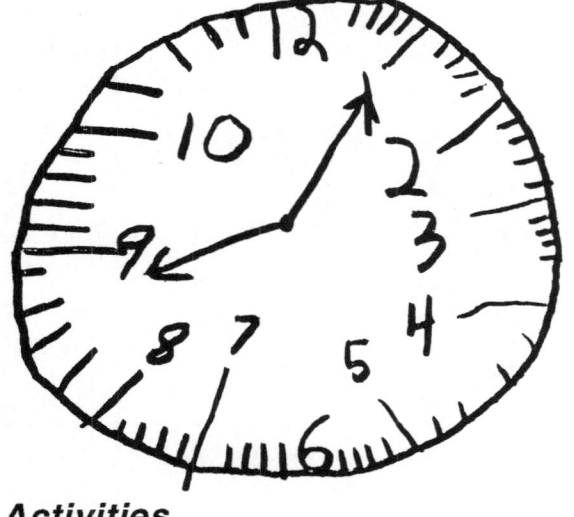

This party is for people who like to dance and have a good time. Either rent a juke box or use your own stereo for music. Everyone must dance!

Invitations
- The invitation should resemble the face of a clock with the party information located inside.
- Ask your guests to bring a gift the couple can use, for example, "between 8:00 am and 9:00 am" (the guest might bring a waffle iron or a coffee maker). Make sure the entire day is covered from breakfast to bedtime.

Activities
While the guests are dancing, the host should ring a bell to resemble a clock chiming. Each time the bell rings, the dancing should stop and the guest who brought a gift for the time of day that is rung should present it to the guests of honor.

112

Couch Potato Shower

Invitations
- Purchase or make small pillows and write invitation with permanent markers.
- Very casual dress - sweatsuits, etc.

Menu
Recipes using potatoes - potato skins, potato salad, potato soup, potato chips, potato pancakes. Remember, vodka is made from potatoes!

Gifts
CD's and videotapes of favorite movies, cassettes, books, and crossword puzzles.

Activities
- Potato Race: Form teams for a relay race. Hold a potato on a large spoon and run.
- Or, if too tired, watch a video concert or movie while sitting on couches eating.

113

Lean on Me Shower

This is a shower for close friends to share together. This get-together is when the guests tell the bride that "we'll be there with you, for help and support, in your new life." It is frightening to make such a drastic change in one's life, so this is the time to tell your friend that she has a family of friends who will be there for her.

Invitations
- Tell guests to bring gifts of their time. For example, four hours of housecleaning, unpacking, lining cabinets, etc. They will know what she needs. Suggest a gift certificate for a manicure, facial, or massage.
- Ask guests to bring memories or pictures of events that they have shared with the bride that will make everybody laugh.

Activities
- Play background music that the bride enjoyed while growing up.
- Pass out a recipe card and pen to each guest. Tell them to write down their favorite recipe for a happy marriage. This can be humorous as well as serious advice. Collect the cards and read aloud without revealing author's name.

114

So They Eloped

Welcome the couple home from the honeymoon with a surprise shower. Ask the couple to bring wedding and honeymoon photos. Invite relatives and friends.

Decorations
Hang banners that read "welcome home" and "just married." Get pictures from the bride and groom's past and put them on posters around the room.

Gifts
Things for the bathroom: towels, soaps, robes, etc.

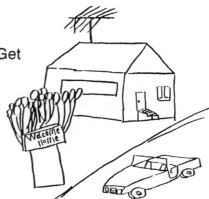

115

Wine and Cheese Shower

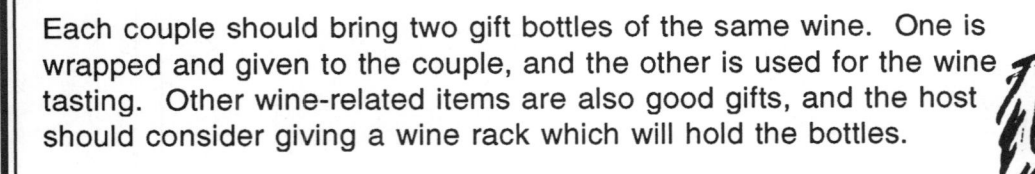

Each couple should bring two gift bottles of the same wine. One is wrapped and given to the couple, and the other is used for the wine tasting. Other wine-related items are also good gifts, and the host should consider giving a wine rack which will hold the bottles.

Invitations
Write the invitation on a plastic wineglass with a permanent marker. Hand deliver the glass or send it in a box lined with tissue paper.

Menu
Serve French bread, crackers, fruit, cheese, and soda.

Activities
Before each wine is tasted, have guests offer a toast to the wedding couple.

116

Be My Valentine Shower

Plan a Valentine's shower any time of the year. Everyone loves this holiday and will enjoy the memory.

Invitations

- Write them on Valentine's cards. If you are lucky to have your shower around Valentine's Day, use children's valentines; otherwise, make your own.
- Guests should bring gifts that will help the bride build a loving home. Each gift should have a note explaining "why this gift will make your home more loving." The gifts can be serious or humorous.

Activities

Sweetheart Match: Pass around a piece of paper and have everyone write something unique about their own courtship or wedding without revealing their identity. Have the bride read each and have guests guess who wrote each passage.

Menu

Serve heart-shaped sandwiches and cookies and red punch.

117

Breakfast Shower

Invitations
- Schedule a late-morning brunch.
- Tell guests to wear pajamas or nightgowns.
- Gifts should reflect the theme and be cooking items used for preparing breakfast, or a gift certificate to a favorite restaurant that serves breakfast.

Activities
Create a Book: Use plain white paper for pages and make a cover that resembles a house. Pass the book around and have everyone write their hints for a happy home!

Menu
Serve a brunch accompanied by coffee, tea, and champagne.

Decorations
- Have floral arrangements and morning newspaper on table.
- Play classical music and enjoy a leisurely morning of good food and good friends.

118

Picnic Barbeque Shower

This is a great shower in which to present a group gift of a gas barbeque grill, an ice cream maker, etc.

If there is a park close by, follow the shower with a softball game or kite flying. Kites can be provided by the host as a party favor.

Decorations
Decorate your yard as if you were at the beach or a park. If the party needs to be indoors, use red-and-white checkered tablecloths and sit on the floor.

Activities
Have yard games such as croquet and volleyball.

Menu
Barbeque an assortment of fish, hamburgers, chicken, and sausages. Serve with salad and pie.

119

Cookbook Shower

Good cooking is the key to this party! This is a great shower idea for co-workers or neighbors to give.

Invitations
- With each invitation, send a "gourmet" recipe for the guest to prepare for the party.
- Set up a buffet and place the recipe card next to each dish. Following the meal, place the recipes in a recipe card holder and give it to the guest of honor.
- The host or hostess should wear a cooking apron when answering the door.
- A great group gift might be a certificate for a gourmet cooking class. Individuals can give a copy of their favorite cookbook.

Decorations
Decorate with the cooking theme in mind. Flour and sugar bowls can be used as centerpieces on table. Rent a Julia Child cooking video tape and have it playing during the shower.

120

Honeymoon Shower

Invitations
Send invitations asking couples to dress in a manner appropriate to the location of the honeymoon. For example, if the bride and groom are planning to go to Hawaii, have a luau, or if it is Asia, have a Chinese dinner!

Decorations
Try to decorate according to their destination. Go to the library and borrow a record or tape that has music from that city or country.

Menu
Plan a dinner that fits with the theme and is creative.

Gifts
Things to use on their honeymoon, or money.

121

Couple's Kitchen Shower

Invitations
- Purchase two inexpensive aprons for each invited couple. Write the party information on each with a permanent marker.
- Tell guests they must wear their invitation to the party!
- Gifts should be kitchen items.

Menu
Plan a meal so that each couple has to make something. Place necessary ingredients and recipe cards for each dish on counter for couples to use. The recipes should be simple and fast.

Decorations
- Decorate the table with mixing bowls, measuring cups, blenders, etc.
- Play music while chefs prepare dinner. Put name cards on buffet table marking who made each dish.

122

Gift Display Get Together

This is a great get together for friends and relatives a few days before the wedding takes place. Have shower in the late afternoon or after dinner.

Decorations
Display gifts by category. Do not place modest gifts by expensive gifts, and place checks in a white envelope with the name of donor on front. Set gifts on dining room table, and allow guests to browse at their leisure. If this shower includes the wedding party, it is a nice time for the bride to present her gifts and to say something special about each person.

Menu
Serve tea or coffee and a choice of two or three beautiful cakes.

123

Garden Tea Shower

Activities

Hire someone to demonstrate flower arranging. Everyone will learn a new skill and enjoy themselves at the same time!

Decorations

- Have a potted plant as a centerpiece on the dining table.
- Have each guest write down a question for the bride on a piece of paper and tie it to plant. Before she opens the gifts, she must answer each question.

Invitations

- Tell guests to wear their favorite hat!
- Gift ideas should be gardening tools, magazine subscriptions, bulbs, plants, shrubs, and house plants. A group gift might be a wheelbarrow or lawn furniture.
- Gift certificate to a local nursery.

Menu

Prepare an English tea. Make small sandwiches of egg, crab, and tuna salad. Cut off crusts and cut into small squares and triangles. Serve cookies, scones, muffins, and petit fours.

124

Entertainment Shower for Couples

Most newlyweds are saving for something such as a house, a car, or furniture. They don't save for things that would allow them to spend time together and to have fun. Give the couple a shower featuring entertainment accessories. The theme of this party should be "games."

Invitations
• Make the invitation to resemble a ticket with the party information inside.
• Ask guests to bring gifts of games, records, memberships (to museums, zoos, or art galleries), and tickets (for the theatre, a sporting event, or a concert).

Activities
• Hire a ballroom dance instructor to teach your guests. This way, the guests will be prepared to dance at the wedding reception!
• Roll dice to see who dances with whom.

125

Christmas Shower

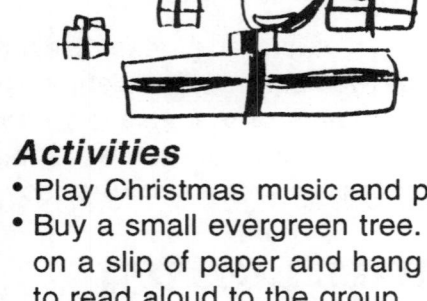

It doesn't have to be Christmas time to share Christmas cheer! Christmas decorations are expensive, and most newlyweds don't have them. Give gifts of Christmas ornaments, decorations, and accessories.

Invitations
• Write invitation inside a Christmas card.
• Tell guests to wear festive clothing.

Menu
Serve your traditional Christmas buffet with cookies, cakes, hot chocolate, and cider.

Activities
• Play Christmas music and play a game of charades.
• Buy a small evergreen tree. Have each guest write something to the couple on a slip of paper and hang it on the tree. The couple can choose which ones to read aloud to the group.

126

This is Your Life Shower

This shower will take some planning in advance, but the results are worth the effort.

Invitations
Inform each guest to come dressed (you may have to supply some outfits) as part of the bride's past.

Activities
Set up a treasure hunt for the bride which should start at the bride's house. Have the bride's and groom's mothers drive her to each destination. Give the bride several clues telling her the location of each stop. Guests will be at each location, and will tell her about the time of her life according to the costume they are wearing. The hunt will continue until she reaches the last stop where all the guests have gathered to have food and fun.

127

Some Enchanted Evening

Romance is on the rise! Set the mood for the new couple's future by having a romantic shower.

Decorations
• Decorate the area with flowers and use candles for the lighting.
• Play romantic music or hire a pianist or harpist.

Menu
Serve an elegant dinner and use fine china and silver.

Gifts
Things that smell good: potpourri, scented candles, drawer liners, gift certificates from florists so bride can have fresh flowers for a month or a year.

128

Secret Undercover Agent Party

Have two separate surprise Bridal and Groom showers on the same night. Mystery kidnapping at the end of each shower will bring both parties together for refreshments.

Invitations
- Undercover agent theme.
- Request all guests to wear sunglasses, hats, and trench/raincoats over casual dress.
- Gift items should be all "undercover" items, i.e., lingerie for bride-to-be and underclothing for the groom. Matching robes might be given by the group.

Activities
Each "secret agent" must illustrate his/her investigative qualities by telling a story of how they imagine the bride and groom's first date, kiss, dance, fight, etc. went. Be sure to have a tape or video recorder on. Towards the end of the showers arrange to have the couple "kidnapped" from their respective showers and taken to another home. After the "kidnapping" distribute "Clue Lists" to the undercover agents (guests) and the hunt begins.

When the bride and groom are discovered the search ends, refreshments are served, and a prize may be given to the "Agent" who first makes the discovery.

129

True Value Friends

This is a party theme with a masculine touch. It is a hardware shower, providing the couple with many practical gifts.

Invitations
- Tell guests to come dressed in overalls or work pants. Have two pairs of overalls ready for the bride and groom to wear when they arrive.
- Have guests meet at a local hardware store an hour before the party. Everyone can have fun shopping together and duplicate gifts will be avoided.

Decorations
Use centerpieces made of fresh vegetables and flowers displayed in colorfully painted pipe joints. Place gifts in a large laundry basket with balloons tied to them. The couple can use the hamper to transport their gifts.

Activities
Provide each guest with a 3 x 5 card on which to write handy hints. Have each guest read his or her hints aloud and place cards in a card file for the couple to take home.

Menu
Order a submarine sandwich that can be divided easily. Order a cake to be made in the shape of a tool.

130

Cookie Sampler for Mother

This is a very social and casual party for the mother of either the bride or the groom.

Invitations
- Invite a group of the mother's friends, relatives, and neighbors.
- The invitation should be in the shape of a large cookie.
- Request each guest to bring their favorite cookie dough, a baking sheet, and a copy of the recipe for the guest of honor. Cookies to be baked at party.
- Shower gifts for the bride and groom might be cookie cutters, baking sheets, baking equipment, and mixing bowls.

Decorations
Have bright, colorful, festive balloons, streamers, and fresh flower arrangements.

Menu
Serve juice, coffee, tea, and milk with the cookies as they come out of the oven. Wrap and freeze all extra cookies for the mother's freezer. These will be handy to serve to guests during the wedding weekend.

131

Let's Fill the Freezer Party

This shower is for a second marriage, or when moving into a new place.

Invitations
- Save frozen food containers and clean them.
- Place invitation to party on a printed sheet inside containers.
- Request that guests bring homemade, freezer-ready items to the guest of honor.
- Label each item and bring its recipe to place in a recipe file.
- Suggestions: Spaghetti sauce, all kinds of soups and stews, baked goods, jams and jellies.

Menu
Serve frozen gourmet T.V. dinners, frozen desserts, and beverages.

Activities
Shower Game: Each guest tells story of how they met the guest of honor and their first impressions (a form of Truth or Dare). If participants do not think it is the true story a dare must be picked from the dare box. Dares can be "sing a song," dance to a certain record, stand on one leg for 3 minutes, etc. Dare box is made by each party guest writing down and placing their dare in box before game begins.

132

Here Comes the "Brides"

Invitations
Copy a black and white picture of a bride and groom. Glue to construction paper and fold in half. Write party information on the inside.

Decorations
• Everyone (except the bride to be) must come in their wedding dress. If unmarried, dress as a bridesmaid. Most women should be excited to have a chance to wear their wedding dress again!
• Ask guests to bring wedding photos.

Activities
• Choose three wedding songs. Give each guest a copy of one of the songs. Everyone with the same song gets together for a few moments to practice their songs for the group. For fun and confusion, try singing all three songs at the same time.
• Make sure to take pictures to give each "bride."

Menu
Wedding cake, champagne or fruit punch, and finger food.

133

Times Past - Neighborhood Reunion

Invitations
- Take a photograph of a local store, restaurant, or park in your old neighborhood. Make photocopies and use for front of invitation.
- Ask guests to bring current pictures of their families and homes. Display on walls, or in albums.
- Contact a restaurant to reserve a party room.

Decorations
Decorate party area with pictures, posters, and newspapers from the days when you lived in the area.

Activities
Play music of the time period you are celebrating.

Menu
Offer a simple meal, and allow each family to pay for their own.

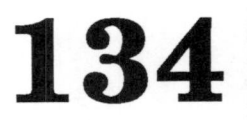

134

Sports Parents Reunion

If you have or had children on a sports team, this is the party for you!

Invitations
- Photocopy the front of a sports program and place the invitation inside.
- Invite parents only!
- Request guests to bring videotapes and photos of their children's "teams."
- Dress should be items or shirts worn during "sports fan days."

Menu
Serve a large pot of fresh stew with garlic bread, cake, and beverages. Or, have a potluck and assign dishes for guests to bring.

135

"M.A.S.H." Farewell Party

This is a party for those die-hard fans of the movie and television series, "M.A.S.H."

Invitations
Request guests to wear their favorite "M.A.S.H." character's garb and to be prepared to tell and act out some of their favorite scenes.

Decorations
• Borrow marine equipment to set up a M.A.S.H. unit in your backyard or garage.
• Go to an army/navy surplus store to purchase camouflage items, netting, tents, and water pistols.

Menu
Serve sloppy joes, hot dogs, baked beans, and hamburgers. Use mess kits and tin cups for utensils.

136

Gallery Hopping Video Shows

Invitations
Invite your neighbors for an impromptu evening of art gallery hopping using videos on artists' works. (These videos are usually available through art libraries or galleries.)

Decorations
Have supporting books and information about artists and their works.

Menu
Serve finger sandwiches with fruit punch, mimosas, fresh fruit with honey and cookies.

137

Lawn Christening Party

This party is for new lawn owners.

Invitations
- Use artificial turf or remnants of green carpet cut into small shapes. This can be found at a hardware or lawn store.
- Staple paper containing party information to backside of carpet.
- Dress should be casual or perhaps lawn clothes of the roaring twenties!

Menu
An outdoor buffet featuring southern fried chicken and pink lemonade.

Games
Choose teams and play croquet, darts, lawn bowling, and badminton. For prizes, offer lawn care certificates and other lawn supplies!

138

October Harvest Potluck

Invitations
- Invite guests via telephone.
- Ask friends to bring a "harvest" from their vegetable gardens
  or favorite produce garden store.

Menu
You should provide the soup's stock base, rolls, salad, dessert,
and beverages. Guests can help toss the salad while others are
preparing their vegetables for the soup.

Decorations
Fresh flowers from your garden in beautiful arrangements.

Activities
- Play soft, romantic background
  music.
- Buy dried straw wreaths from craft
  store and decorate with dried or silk
  flowers, birds, etc.

139

New Pet Owners Shower

Invitations
- Glue pictures of pets on a folded card.
- Include a list of pet needs and size and type of guest of honor (let the new pet be the "star").
- Invite a local pet expert who will present a short talk on pet care and other pet information.

Decorations
Pet posters, pet accessories with flowers as centerpieces.

Activities
- Have a pet fashion show.
- Vote on which owners look the most like their pet!

Menu
Serve a casual menu consisting of deli sandwiches and chips.

140

Extended Dinner Party

- This idea is for new neighbors or a neighbor with a new baby. It provides a relaxing dinner to become acquainted with each other and freedom from dinner preparation for the new neighbor over a period of several weeks.
- Call the existing neighbors that are interested in hosting a dinner and arrange a schedule for the dinner parties over several weeks. These dinners can be individual with the hosts and new couple, or involve more than two couples.

Invitations

Phone the guests of honor and follow-up with written invitations with the schedule of dinners from all of the neighbors. R.S.V.P. will be very helpful.

Activities

- Good food, good conversation, and testing of different menus.
- Hosts may provide guests with copies of recipes used for the dinner.

141

Games Galore

Invitations
- Invite all of your friends (all ages) for a "games" party.
- Ask each person to bring their favorite game.
- Upon arrival, ask guests to set up their games.
- Form teams and play games.

Menu
Serve finger foods that will not disturb game-playing.

142

Backyard Croquet Tournament

Organize a croquet tournament in your backyard!

Invitations
• Telephone neighbors and friends, adults and children.

Menu
Serve a casual buffet of deli sandwiches, salads, Jello, lemonade, and cookies.

Activities
• Form teams of two, consisting of an adult and a child.
• Play croquet.
• Offer prizes that will appeal to all ages.

143

Community Clean-Up Party

- Everyone can do their part to clean up the environment. Call your city to find a stream or park that needs to be cleaned. Send flyers to everyone you know to meet at the location on a certain day.
- Invite a friend who can identify different types of plants and flowers for guests to notice while they are cleaning.
- Ask everyone to bring a picnic lunch.

144

Movers Dinner

- Are your neighbors moving? Invite them over for a private family dinner while you and your friends pack their belongings for the move. This will give their family some time alone as the packing continues, so they won't feel guilty for taking a time-out!
- Ask your neighbors to give you a list of instructions on which room to pack, etc. Keep an inventory list of each box's contents for future use.

145

I Once Was A ...

This is a great party for new friends and neighbors. It helps break the ice and gives guests the chance to become acquainted with each other!

Invitations
- Use a square piece of paper and draw a frame around the edge. Draw a question mark in the center of each "frame."
- Ask guests to come dressed in costume which represents something they have done in the past (they should bring a photograph of what they actually looked like at that time!).

Menu
Serve food to go with the era you are representing (for example, if you are a pregnant lady who only drank milkshakes and ate pizza, that is what you will serve!).

146

Places We've Been

This is a travel party. Bring out all your slides, pictures, or films of family vacations or places individual members have visited. Talk about destinations some members may not know about. Serve snacks from different travel locations. If vacations were taken when children were young, tell them what they did on that particular vacation.

169

Movie Madness

Rent a favorite old movie or go together to see a new movie at a theatre. Make popcorn and serve juice. Critique the movie afterwards and discuss its strong and weak points, and how it related to you. Encourage everyone to participate. If you go out to see a movie, take a walk before returning home.

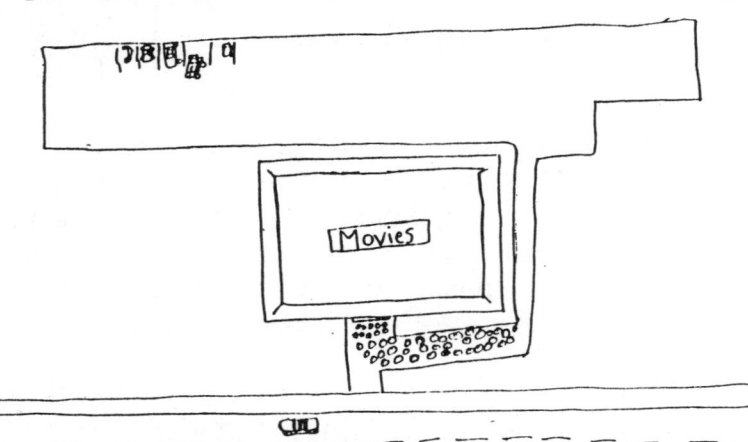

170

Bike Bash

Invite the family to attend a bike ride. Give everyone streamers and tape for decorating their bikes before leaving. The leader will choose where you are going. It is fun to end your ride at a park or lake to enjoy a picnic lunch and a swim.

171

Picture a Potluck

This is a great extended family party, so include the children.

Invitations
Tell guests what category of food they should bring, for example, a salad, main course, dessert, beverage, etc.

Activities
As the guests arrive or during the course of the party, draw each person's silhouette. Use a bright lamp to project their profile on the wall and trace it on a piece of paper; on the back, write the name of the guest. Display the pictures and allow everyone to guess who each one is. The person who guesses the most correctly wins! This is a great way to get everyone to know each other's names. The children will enjoy taking part in the guessing.

172

Roller Blade Binge

This is a great family outing.

Invitations
• Make in the shape of a roller skate.
• Invite guests to bring their roller blades or skates.
• Meet at your house and proceed to a local park with
  a skating path.

Menu
Have a barbeque after the skating. Reserve park grills and invite
guests to bring their own "picnic to grill." You provide the beverages,
dessert, and condiments.

173

Do, Re, Mi, Mi, Mi

Choose a time and date to spend time alone to do something
you enjoy. Just celebrate you!

Activities
A few ideas might be:
- A trip to a spa.
- A massage.
- A sports event.
- A nature hike.
- A long, soothing bath while sipping champagne.
  Indulge yourself. You deserve it!

174

Sundae Social

Invitations
- Have this party on a Sunday.
- Make invitations to resemble the sun.

Activities
- Most creative sundae award.
- Take a nature hike to walk the calories off.

Menu
Serve make-your-own sundaes!

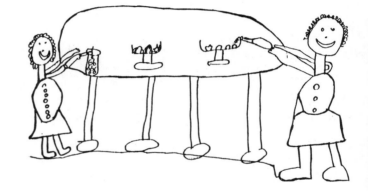

175

Pretzel Party

Invitations
Twist a pipe cleaner into the shape of a pretzel. Write a small invitation and attach it to the pretzel. If you are inviting immediate family members, attach it to their doorknobs!

Activities
• Make pretzels. Try making pretzels shaped to resemble people, houses, etc. and give a prize for the best design.
• While pretzels are baking, play a game of Twister!

Pretzel recipe (yields 12 pretzels):
You will need 1 tsp. salt, 1 tbsp. active dry yeast, 1 c. hot water, 1/2 c. instant milk powder, 1/4 c. veg. oil, 2 tbsp. honey, 1 1/2 c. flour, 1 tsp. baking soda, 1/2 c. yogurt. Mix first seven ingredients and cover to let rise for one hour. Add additional items and let rise. Knead, divide into 10 parts, and roll into 1/2" long snakes. Shape and bake at 350 degrees for 10 minutes or until brown.

176

"How Does Your Garden Grow?" Party

This party is fun for a wedding shower, anniversary, or housewarming party.

Invitations

- Roll up invitation into a scroll and place in colorful cloth garden gloves. Mail or hand deliver to homes.
- Invite guests to bring garden equipment, plants, or flower bulbs which will be gifts for the guest of honor.
- Hold party in private garden for a nominal charge by calling city hall in advance.

Games

- Garden Trivia Questions: Form teams to answer trivia questions written in advance on cards.
- Wheelbarrow Races: Form couples. One person rides in wheelbarrow, while other pushes from start to finish line.
- Sack Races: Form teams to race a relay while wearing sacks over legs.

Decorations

Tape brightly colored floral fabrics to tabletops. Use red clay flower pots to fill with fruits, flowers, and vegetables as centerpieces. Garden equipment can be set around party area as decoration too!

Menu

Deli box lunches including turkey, ham, beef, corned beef and cheese sandwiches. Also, have fruit, potato chips, and cookies. Use a wheelbarrow to fill with ice and beverages.

177

Everybody's All-American Party

- Plan party on day of a "big game" (football, hockey, baseball, etc.).
- Meet at host's house for appetizers.
- Rent a school bus to transport guests to event.
- After sports event, return to party for dinner.

Invitations
Copy a sports page from a newspaper, but substitute the headlines with party information. It may be possible to purchase these at novelty stores.

Decorations
- Decorate party area with pom-poms, streamers, balloons, pennants, posters, etc.
- Have team songs as background music.

Menu
Serve chili, corn bread, fruit salad, vegetable tray, and assorted beverages. For dessert, serve make-your-own sundaes.

178

"Memories of Lace" Tea Party

This is an easy afternoon tea party to celebrate the young woman graduate. Invite friends and their mothers!

Invitations
- Use lace remnants; glue or stitch on satin-sheen paper. Attach satin pastel-colored ribbon to front of folded card.
- Ask each guest to recite a story about the guest of honor during party.

Decorations
- Place lace cloth on tables and use fine china and silver tea service (this can be rented).
- Display a photo collage of guest of honor.
- Place fresh flower arrangements with candles on tables.

Menu
Serve cucumber and tomato, watercress, and egg-salad finger sandwiches. For dessert, serve ice cream, cake, nuts, mints, tea, and coffee.

179

Leaving for College Shower

This is a party to prepare the guests of honor for their years in college and could be held for several students.

Invitations
Send invitations to friends and relatives with a "wish and need list." The gifts do not have to be new! The guests may bring an item that they own and do not use any longer.

Decorations
Use a college theme and decorate room with logos, pennants, and school colors.

Menu
Offer casual and simple food. You can barbeque hamburgers and hot dogs. Serve with soft drinks and salads.

180

Opening Day of Fishing Season Party

Surprise your favorite fisher-person by inviting their fishing friends to an early morning breakfast before departing for the first day of fishing.

Invitations
Cut out fish shapes in heavy paper and write details of party on front.

Decorations
Place fishing equipment around party area. Hang maps and posters of lakes.

Games
Take turns telling fish stories.

181

So It's Final (party for the newly divorced)

Divorce is an emotionally straining time in your friend's life. Why not cheer up your friend with a surprise party!

Invitations
Arrange party in advance so guests can shop for luxurious gifts that the guest of honor would never buy for her/himself (for example, a day at a salon or fitness club, a massage, etc.).

Decorations
- Use a candyland motif. Hang colorful balloons and streamers on walls and place candy on tables.
- For centerpieces, tie several balloons to a weight and place in a small colored bag. Stuff colorful tissue around top of bag and glue candy to outside of bag.
- Play upbeat background music.
- Send guests home with a small box of chocolates.

Games
Go to a local bowling alley. Form teams and play a few games!

182

Wedding Rehearsal Dinner

Are you on a wedding budget? Here's a great idea.

Invitations
Enlist family members and friends to prepare, serve, and clean up a potluck dinner at parents' home. Other ideas:
• Picnic at local parks.
• Barbeque at parks or family members' home.

Menu
Allow the mothers of bride and groom to select a desirable menu. Assign various guests different tasks and dishes to bring.

183

Election Night Results Party

This is a great party if you have a friend who is running for office. If not, just pretend!

Invitations
• Use red, white, and blue paper.
• Do not start party too early. Have plenty of T.V.s and radios playing.

Games
Collect newspapers. Get partners. Have one person design and one person model. Vote for the best inaugural outfit.

Menu
Offer a simple deli buffet including sandwiches, fruit, cheese, and beverages. For dessert, prepare cupcakes with miniature American flags on top.

Decorations
• Have red, white, and blue straw hats on tables.
• Hang donkey and elephant cardboard posters on walls.
• Have bullhorns to announce the election results.
• Hang campaign posters on walls.
• Play historical campaign music softly (this may be found at a local library on tape).

184

"Out-of-Town Guests" Wedding Breakfast

This event serves several good purposes. It frees the wedding family so they can prepare for the wedding, and out-of-town guests can meet and visit with each other before the wedding.
This party can be your wedding gift.

Invitations
• Have a breakfast brunch for all out-of-town guests the morning of the wedding.
• Secure from bride a list of names and addresses.
• Send invitation before guests arrive in town.
• A luncheon can be served if wedding takes place in the evening.

185

Purple and Red Hat Retirement Party

Invitations

• These should read: When I am an old woman, I shall wear purple with a red hat which doesn't go and doesn't suit me, and I shall spend my pension on brandy and summer gloves and satin sandals and say we've no money for butter. I shall sit down on the pavement when I'm tired and gobble up samples in stores and press alarm bells and run my stick along the public railings and make up for the sobriety of my youth.

I shall go out in my slippers in the rain and pick flowers in other people's gardens and learn to spit...but maybe I ought to practice a little now? So people who know me are not too shocked and surprised when suddenly I am old and start to wear purple. ("Warning" by Jenny Joseph)

Please join us at the retirement party of ...... Please wear purple and red only!

Games

Have guests tell stories about guest of honor such as when they first met, amusing incidents, etc.

Menu

Serve red cranberry punch, retirement cake, ice cream, nuts, mints, and red Jello.

Gift Suggestions

Red hat, purple gifts, slippers, Irish Creme liquor, Creme de Menthe, satin sandals, and brandy.

Decorations

Have purple and red balloons, pictures and posters of retiree.

186

Hunting Send-Offs

This is a party to celebrate the new hunting season with your favorite hunters.

Invitations
Mail several weeks in advance. Request guests to bring prepared dishes and casseroles for the hunters to take with them.

Menu
A casual dinner consisting of a large pot of stew served with wine and beer. Also trail mix snacks.

Games
Tell hunting stories while sitting by the fireplace.

Once the hunting party arrives at their cabin, all they will have to concentrate on is "bagging their limit!" They will not have to spend time on preparing meals.

187

May I Have Your Autograph, Please?

This is an end of the school year autograph party for students aged 12-18 years old.

Invitations
- Contact guests and ask for a baby or childhood photograph; use these as decorations. Be sure to put identification on the backs of photographs. Have guests guess who they are.
- Inform guests that they should bring their yearbooks for signing.

Menu
Serve pizza, cola, and fudge brownies for dessert.

Decorations
- Use school colors and memorabilia such as sports pennants, jerseys, and past yearbooks. Megaphones and pom-poms will make great centerpieces.
- Contact the yearbook photographer and ask for photographs of the students. Paste them onto posterboard and hang on walls.
- For background music, play the popular tunes of the past year.

188

Post-Wedding Send-Off Brunch

This brunch is for out-of-town relatives and the newlyweds. It takes place the morning after the wedding, allowing time for the relatives to visit with the bride and the groom before they leave for the honeymoon. It is also a good opportunity for the couple to open relatives' gifts.

Menu
Items can be prepared several days in advance, or hire a caterer. Egg souffles and fruit salad would be nice.

Send the bride and groom off with a picnic basket filled with champagne, juices, fruit, sandwiches, wedding cake, and crystal glasses.

189

A Jug of Wine, A Loaf of Bread and Thou

A private engagement party for two.

Invitations
- Use a floral motif.
- Men should invite their fiancées to a private picnic in a romantic location, such as a beach or garden.

Menu
Fill picnic basket with wine, bread, cheese, fruit, and a diamond ring.

Remember to bring a tape player (for sweet background music) and a picnic blanket.

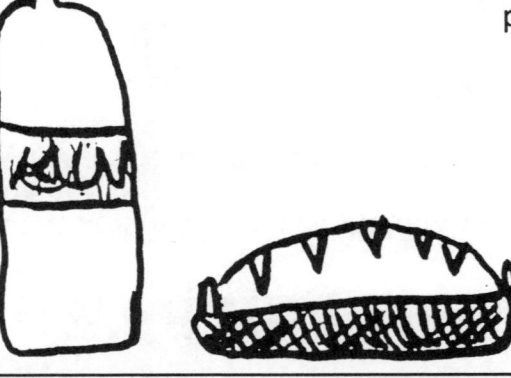

190

And Here's .... Party

This is a graduation party for teens or adults. It should not be a surprise. A roast will occur in which the guests tell humorous stories about the graduate. (You can also use this theme for wedding showers, anniversaries, and retirements.) Ask guests to bring or send photos and written memories of the graduate. Place these in a scrapbook which will be presented to the guest of honor. For the grand finale, show a slide show or video about the graduate's life.

Invitations

- You will need to plan this party well in advance. Invite friends, relatives, and past acquaintances of the guest of honor, but keep the guest list a secret.
- Hold the party just before or after graduation day.
- Cut construction paper into rectangles. Print information, roll into a scroll, and tie it with ribbon. Use a gold or silver ink pen for a special effect.

Decorations

- Have a picture board of graduate, and graduation party theme paper products. Hang balloons and streamers in the school colors. Set up a "stage" area for the "roast" with a chair for the graduate.
- Choose appropriate songs to accompany the "memories" told by guests. Be sure to videotape the roast!

191

Hawaiian Wedding Anniversary Party

Treat your guests to a "mini" Hawaiian vacation. Call a dance school and hire a teacher for hula instruction. Teach your guests to strum the ukulele and sing Polynesian songs.

Invitations
- Request guests to wear Hawaiian dress, and to bring bathing suits.
- Greet each guest with a flower lei and a kiss of welcome.
- Have party poolside and place straw mats on the grass for guests to sit on.

Decorations
Use Hawaiian and island fare and display coconuts and fruit arrangements on tables.

Menu
Serve a luau buffet featuring sweet and sour dishes, roasted ham, fresh fruit salad, and fruit drinks with pineapple sticks.

192

Let's Dance at Home Party

Many people love to dance, but seem to wait for a special occasion that happens only a few times a year. This party will give them the opportunity to dance. Some good excuses could be: 25th Silver Anniversary (or any other anniversary), fully paid-off mortgage party, or last child off to school.

Decorations
Decorate the party area with glitter and silver streamers and balloons. Hang spotlights and place candles on tables.

Music
Good sound is the key to a successful party. Have upbeat live or recorded music that has a good rhythm to keep the guests dancing. You should consult with a disc jockey or a band leader for appropriate musical choices.

Menu
Dinner should be light because of the amount of exercise. Have plenty of cold refreshments available.

193

All-Night Graduation Party

This large graduation party will keep the happy graduates from drinking and driving on their big night. It will last all night and finish with a breakfast. The parents plan the party, decorations, and food and also chaperone the event. May be held at school. There is one rule: Once a graduate enters the party they must stay until breakfast. If they wish to leave, they must be escorted home by their parents.

Invitations
- First send a notice to all parents asking them to volunteer for one task on your party list, i.e., entertainment, food, decorations, prizes, games, transportation, security, breakfast, set-up, and clean-up.
- Indicate the price (students who are unable to afford the party are excepted), and the check will be the R.S.V.P.

Menu
Serve hot dogs, pizza, popcorn, ice cream, cookies, soda, and milk. Local merchants and parents are usually willing to donate items.

Games
Mini golf, bingo, game shows, frisbee toss, video games, short movies, and popular music (dance band or D.J.).

Decorations
The planning committee should select a theme. For example: Western, Peanuts, Showboat, Back to the Future, Game Shows, Casino, etc.

194

By the Light of the Moon

This party is best for couples and should be held during the fall. It can also double as a Halloween party with the proper decorations and costumes.

Invitations
- Cut construction paper into large moons.
- Print information on one side.
- Have party during a full moon.
- Request couples to write a story of how they first met. This will be read by someone else and no names will be announced.
- Rent a hayride and driver for a 30-minute ride.

Menu
Take a cooler full of beverages on hayride and serve box dinners afterwards.

Games
- Read stories of first encounters aloud and let guests guess whose it is.
- Bring a tape recorder for romantic background music during hayride.

195

Four-Legged Frolic

Invite all your dog-loving friends and their dogs.

Invitations
Purchase small rubber doggie bone toys and tie paper invitation on it with yarn. You may also cut out photographs of dogs from magazines and glue to cardboard and print information on reverse.

Game
Have each guest tell favorite story about their dog, or have dog do favorite "trick."

Menu
Cheese hot dogs, potato salad, pasta salad, vegetable tray and dip, bone-shaped brownies, soft drinks, and for the dogs, doggie treats, water in bowls.

196

Over 60 Love-Tennis Party

A mixed doubles tournament on Valentine's Day.

Invitations
- Reserve your tennis courts for February 14th.
- Send heart-shaped invitations.
- Request guests to wear red and white outfits.

Activities
The doubles teams will be picked by exchanging valentines with numbers on the back. Play a round robin tournament. After tennis is completed, serve refreshments or return to your home for a buffet meal. The winners should receive a heart-shaped box of chocolates and a bottle of champagne.

197

Condo Pool Party

Reserve the pool area at your apartment or condo complex. Rope off an area for gift-opening and refreshments.

Invitations
- Purchase small inflatable inner tubes in different shapes. Write your invitation on these with a permanent marker. Deflate and mail in envelopes.
- Suggest guests come in swimming suits, and bring sporty clothes and shoes.

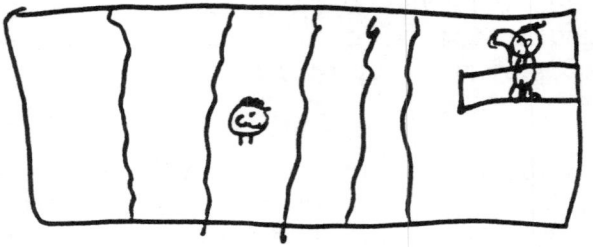

Decorations
Decorate pool area with balloons and write birthday guests' names on them.

Activities
- Water balloon fight, water volleyball.
- Play "water" theme music.

198

Local PGA Golf Tournament

Reserve a tee time at a local golf course to coincide with the "hallowed" PGA tourney. Enlist the help of a golf pro to set up a tournament for you and your guests.

Activities
- Videotape your guests as they play, for viewing during a simple buffet served at the club or your home.
- Play should be best ball mixed couples.
- Closest to pin and shortest drive, longest drive, longest putt.
- Prizes should be golf items (these may be gag gifts if you choose).

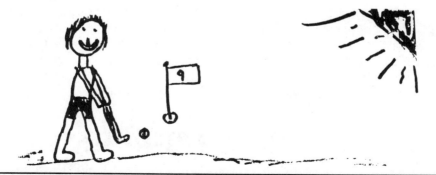

199

Singular Celebrations

Do not forget a friend who has recently lost his/her mate or whose mate is ill and in the hospital.

Invite the person over for dinner. Make it a special day by inviting other friends and relatives to share in the festivities. You can cheer them up and ease their loneliness by just caring and giving the gift of your time. Perhaps you can arrange to visit their bedridden spouse also! Have lots of flowers and balloons.

200

Fish Away!

This is a great surprise party for a man. It is a great idea for a fishing enthusiast. Arrange for a rental or borrowed boat and equipment. Invite friends and relatives who enjoy fishing.

Activities
- Photograph fishermen.
- Have a contest for the biggest and smallest fish caught.
- Float an old tire in the water and allow each guest five attempts to cast their flies or bait in the center.

Menu
Have a shore lunch of fresh salads, baked potatoes, grilled corn on the cob, and grill the catch of the day. Buy a few fish just in case.

201

Come As You Are Breakfast

Call your guests early in the morning and invite them over for breakfast, dressed as they are!

Activities
• Prize for first arrival.
• Prize for most authentic.
• Newspapers to read.

Menu
Baked egg dish, fruit salad, caramel rolls, hot coffee, tea, and hot chocolate.

202

Mardi Gras Party for Grandma

Mardi Gras is a pre-Lenten party in which people wear festive costumes and parade about to lively music.

Bring Mardi Gras to Grandma and her friends! Pre-arrange with nursing home the time, date, menu, etc. of your party. Most places are very cooperative and happy to provide party rooms, kitchen facilities, and supervision. Tell guests to wear fun, colorful outfits.

Decorations
Decorate party room to resemble New Orleans during Mardi Gras.

Activities
- Bring plain party masks and sequins, feathers, glitter, and glue for guests to use in creating their own masks for a parade.
- Have a costume contest, play bingo, and have a cakewalk with music.

203

Spring Concert Sing-a-Long

Call a local college or high school to enlist the help of a choral or band group to help you give a party for a senior citizens' home in your area. Arrange a time and date for the party with the home's director. Discuss room size, number of guests, etc.

Decorations
Decorate the party area with balloons and fresh flowers.
Offer a flower to each guest as they leave.

Activities
• Invite guests who sing or play an instrument to join the choir or band.
• Take Polaroid photographs and give to guests when party is over.

Menu
Have a high tea with homemade treats to enjoy after the concert.

204

Bring a Friend to a Bingo Party

What is more fun than yelling BINGO! and collecting a prize in front of your friends? Plan a Bingo party around a luncheon.

Invitations
- Call or send cardboard Bingo cards with invitation glued to opposite side.
- Tell guests to invite one new friend.
- Ask guests to call in regrets only.

Activities
Play Bingo and offer a prize for each round.

Menu
Serve a simple salad, fresh baked muffin, and Jello salad. Have cookies or brownies for dessert with coffee and tea.

205

Quilting Bee Give-a-Way

Invitations
- Invite friends over who enjoy quilting.
- On front of invitation, attach a picture of a finished quilt; inside include the pattern of the square (or two) that you want them to complete before the party (you should give several months' advance notice for this party).

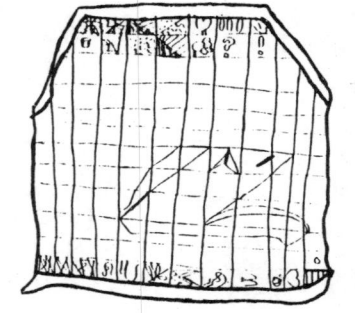

Activities
Have all guests bring their "pieces" and spend the day piecing and sewing them together. Give the completed quilt to a local charity or pick names out of hat for winner.

Menu
Serve a continental breakfast. You may wish to have guests bring a bag lunch. Provide beverages and dessert.

206

Cruise Party Theme

Invitations
- Invitation should resemble identification and embarking passes.
- Write party information inside. Guests must present the embarking card to enter party.

Decorations
- Use a nautical motif with orange life jackets, rubber life boats (fill with ice and beverages), ropes, netting, oars, etc.
- Have a photographer at entry to "ship" to take pictures of guests as they arrive.
- Have signs directing passengers to various areas on ship (B Deck, Port Side, etc.).

Activities
- Ping-Pong, checkers, miniature crap and roulette, gin rummy, and other card games.
- End the cruise with a passenger talent show!

Menu
Serve a lavish midnight buffet.

207

Globe Trotter's Party

This is a get-together in which guests are also the hosts! The party moves to each guest's house for an equal period of time. The host at each interval should be in the costume of a chosen country or culture and serve a menu featuring the country's popular dishes. In addition, the house should be decorated appropriately.

For example, if a host chooses Morocco, she should serve koos-koos and dress as a belly dancer. For a French theme, use small tables and cover with checkered tablecloths as in a caberet with background music.

208

Garage Gertie

Invitations
Cut squares from the classified section of the newspaper which features garage sales and glue on cardboard. Print birthday party information inside card.

Decorations
Hang classified advertisements, birthday streamers, and balloons on walls.

Activities
• When guests arrive at party, give each one a shopping bag and a set spending limit ($5.00 or $10.00). Send them off to neighborhood garage sales with a set time limit and specific time to be back at the party house.
• Upon returning to party, each guest must unpack her "finds" and explain why she bought them.
• Gifts will be finds from garage sale hunt.

Menu
If party starts in late morning, serve a hot buffet brunch when shoppers return from garage sales.

209

Golden Wedding Anniversary

This celebration is commemorated with a formal party traditionally hosted by the couple's children.

Invitations

- The guest list should include local and out-of-town family and friends.
- Have an afternoon open house or a tea reception allowing the couple to greet their guests in a relaxed yet festive atmosphere.
- Invitations should be engraved or formally handwritten. Send well in advance for out-of-town guests and include information on accommodations and costs.
- Instead of gifts, ask guests to write, on a sheet of paper, a memory about the couple.
- Compile the memories into a book. This will be treasured by the couple for many years to come.

Decorations

Everything should be in the traditional colors of gold, white, and yellow. Have a golden floral arrangement for a centerpiece. Floral arrangements may include daffodils, yellow roses, chrysanthemums, and any other available golden bloom.

Menu

The menu should be an elegant presentation of foods including a replica of the couple's wedding cake.

210

Coupon Exchange Party

Invitations
Ask guests to bring a specific number of valid coupons to be exchanged at party.

Decorations
Ask a local supermarket manager for discarded posters, flyers, and boxes and use for decorations.

Activities
- Write a list of specific coupons that appear in the flyers from the grocery store. The winner is the one who finds the most and cuts them out first.
- Musical Coupons: Have guests form a circle and pass coupons around as music plays. When music stops, they get to keep the coupon they are holding. Play with one less coupon than the number of people playing the game. The person who is caught without a coupon must leave the game. The rounds continue until there is only one person left in the game.

211

Soup, Soup Everywhere

This is a great party to have during the fall and winter seasons.

Invitations
- Invite guests to bring a pot of their favorite homemade soup and copies of its recipe.
- Guests should dress casually.

Decorations
Have a fire in the hearth and play soft background music.

Activities
- Sit by the fire and tell stories.
- Assemble a collection of the soup recipes to give guests as they leave.

Menu
Host should provide salad, beverages, and dessert.

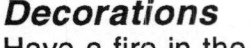

212

Grand Slam Baseball Park Outing

Invitations
- Select a baseball game that will interest guests.
- Make an invitation with a baseball motif.
- Send invitation early and ask for an R.S.V.P.
- You may be able to purchase game tickets at a special group rate.

Activities
Organize a pool and bet on the outcome of the game.

Menu
Serve appetizers and drinks at a tailgate before the game.
You may wish to ask guests to bring something to share.

213

Weekend House Party

Invitations
- Send guests invitations several weeks in advance and request an R.S.V.P.
- Guests should be dressed in casual attire.
- This is an overnight party, so guests should bring extra clothes, etc.

Activities
- Tennis, swimming, sight-seeing, croquet, touch football, etc.
- During the evening, have coffee and dessert and just talk!
- Play various board games and cards.
- Guests can pitch in with the chores.

Menu
Serve a simple soup and salad luncheon. Have a serve-yourself breakfast with cereals, rolls, fruit, coffee, juice, etc.

214

Special Days are Here

When your special seniors are too elderly or infirm, do not forget their special days (birthdays, anniversaries, etc.). They need to be remembered! Plan a wonderful "card shower" to celebrate the special day.

Invitations
Contact relatives, friends, neighbors, and former co-workers with an invitation to write a card or letter to guest of honor. No gifts are necessary, and neither is their presence! The joy of having a card or letter to read can last a long time!

Menu
If immediate family and close friends can attend, serve cake and punch as you shower the cards on the guest of honor!

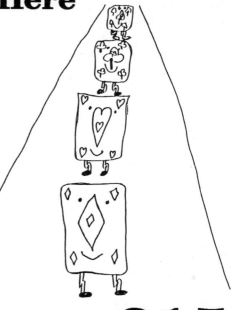

215

Archie Bunker's Bowling Bash

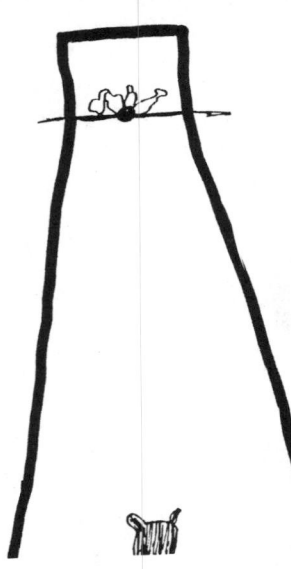

Invitations
- Use blank bowling score sheets for invitations. Ask for an R.S.V.P.
- Arrange with a bowling alley for shoe rentals, food, and lanes (you may be able to bring your own food and beverages).
- Ask guests to dress like Archie and Edith Bunker.
- Meet at host's house and carpool to bowling alley.

Activities
Bowl the evening away and offer winners gift certificates for free bowling.

Menu
You may wish to serve food before or after bowling. Call a sub shop and order an assortment of sandwiches. Serve chips, vegetable and dip trays, and beverages.

216

Crossword Puzzle Party

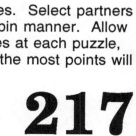

This is a good party to hold in a nursing home or at a senior's apartment.

Invitations
• Glue a crossword puzzle to a card. Write party information inside.
• This party is best when held during the afternoon.

Decorations
Decorate party area with enlarged crossword puzzles, black and white balloons and streamers.

Activities
Place several enlarged crossword puzzles, pencils, and erasers on card tables. Select partners and work on puzzles in teams, while moving from table to table in a round-robin manner. Allow a set amount of time for the teams to work at each table. As the team finishes at each puzzle, they should write their names on it and turn it in to the judge. The team with the most points will win prizes (can be gift certificates to restaurants).

Menu
Serve a light luncheon or a tea during the scoring break.

217

New Year's Day Football

Invitations

Enlist help of friends who will agree to host different parts of the New Year's Day Brunch. Send menus with recipes, suggestions, and timetable, including estimated time when guests will arrive and depart each home.

Progressive Brunch

- Ask guests to wear favorite team's garb.
- Coordinate courses of brunch to start and end with different parades (i.e., Rose Bowl) and football games.
- Games: Set up T.V. for viewing parades and sports. Let guests enter sports pool and guess the winners.
- During half-time, play touch football outside.

218

New Year's Eve Sleigh Ride

Invitations

- Use a sleigh design.
- Tell guests to dress warmly.
- At least one month ahead of time, hire sleigh with a driver and horses.
- Meet at host's house for a hot toddy and hors d'oeuvres. Then, carpool to the sleigh ride stable.

Hopefully, the "full moon" will shine. Start ride around 11:00 pm, so you'll ring the New Year in with the sleigh bells. A romantic evening! Return to a New Year's sunrise breakfast buffet with horns and hats. Adapt your menu so food is cooking and ready on return from sleigh ride.

219

Valentine's Day Singles Party (Adults)

Invitations
Homemade, heart-shaped valentines.

Decorations
- Hearts, cupids, and lace curtains draped around.
- Suspend the hearts from ceiling with clear fishing line.

Games
- As each guest arrives, pin a card onto the back of his or her shirt with one name of a famous couple. Guests must ask questions to find out who they are, so they can identify their lover. This is a good icebreaker and partners can be "lovers" for box suppers or games.
- "Continuous Love Story": Guests sit in a circle while the host starts a story (use a one minute timer). The next person continues the love story until the story is finished to everyone's approval. Tape story to be played back.
- Play musical chairs.
- Have everyone write down what their first date, first kiss, etc. was like. Don't put name on note. Put into a hat. Each guest picks one and takes turns reading.

Menu
"Box Suppers" for two.

220

Cupid Capers Valentines Party

Invitations

You must have 8 to 10 male and female friends who will agree to a "blind date" party. Use heart-shaped red valentines signed by Cupid. Explain "blind date" place and time, etc. Ask each guest to send a description of themselves, including their hobbies and interests. Guests are requested to wear red, semi-formal attire.

Games

- Before the party, the host or hostess matches up the men and women according to descriptions. Upon arrival, the host will hand each person a description of their blind date. Guests walk around asking questions until they find their date.
- Tell-All Game: Pick a subject, set a timer for 3-5 minutes, and have couple tell each other about that subject. For example, animals, past loves, job, etc. Game can go on for as long as the guests are having fun.
- Play your favorite board game.

Menu

Raspberry punch with sherbet. Peanut butter and strawberry heart-shaped sandwiches. Deli sandwiches, chips, Sweetheart white cake, and beverages.

221

I Cannot Tell a Lie - Washington's Birthday

Invitations
Go colonial...flags, red, white and blue bunting or crepe paper streamers, balloons. Cherries and hatchets.

Costumes
Come in colonial dress, such as would be worn by Martha Washington or Paul Revere. Knee breeches, hose, ruffled shirt sleeves, powdered wigs, etc. Have a parade with flags and judge for best costume.

Games
"Nothing But the Truth": Each guest is required to tell the truth to all questions asked in a 2-5 minute time period, or pay a price. (Host to determine penalties.) Each guest takes a turn. Evasive answers or no answer given are also penalized.

Menu
Cherry cobbler with ice cream and beverages or sandwiches with Waldorf salad and cherry Coke with ice cream.

Music
Have a square dance. Hire or recruit a teacher to demonstrate and call the dance. Use recorded calls and music as an alternative.

222

Fasten Your Seat Belt Holiday

Invitations
Use airline ticket jackets (pick up from airlines or travel agent) with pretend tickets inside. Request guests to dress in clothes of their "dream holiday." Don't forget cameras around the neck. Have each guest bring 5-10 favorite holiday slides to party. Host and hostess to dress as pilot and flight attendant.

Location
Arrange to hold party in small local airport area or airport lounge area.

Menu
Serve T.V. dinners or arrange local airline food service to cater party.

Entertainment
Show guests holiday slides throughout the party with music in background.

Games
Famous Tourist Traps: Match up tourist sites and locations. Before party host makes up lists to be matched, i.e., Grand Canyon - Arizona; Disneyland - Los Angeles, California; Delphi - Greece.

223

Groundhog Shadow Party

Invitations
Groundhogs on front. Invite guests to guess time and day when groundhog will see his shadow. Guests should wear only black and white.

Decorations
Have a white bedsheet hanging up with a spotlight behind shape of groundhog.

Favors
Have an artist at party to cut silhouettes of each guest to take home.

Games
Form teams and give 15 to 20 minutes for each team to plan a "shadow" skit behind the sheet. Base each skit on some activity such as playing a sport, robbing a bank, etc. Have audience guess story presented.

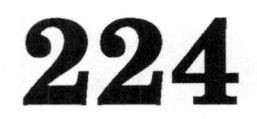

224

Gaelic Sing-a-Long Party

Invitations
Green song sheet with Irish songs on front. Ask guests to "bone up" on Irish songs. Meet at host's house for Irish coffee and a few practice rounds of

Entertainment
Form car/van pool with host's map in hand. Proceed to listed Irish pubs with live music. (This group partying takes advance planning and meeting at pubs with managers to arrange it.) This is a party for Irish only, or those who wish they were Irish.

Game
Ask guests to send a picture of their parents or other "Irish kin" to be hung on the wall upon entering house. The person who matches the most parents to children wins.

Menu
Irish stew or corned beef and cabbage. Crisp shillelaghs (breadsticks), lime sherbet, or pistachio ice cream. Prepare to have dessert on return from "singing tour" or arrange for it to be served at one of the pubs!

225

St. Patrick's Day Party

Invitations
Use a shamrock or Irish motif. Guests should wear green attire.

Games
• St. Patrick's Day limerick contest: Pass out a sheet of examples, such as:
  "There was a young lady from Lynn,
  who was so exceedingly thin
  that when she essayed
  to drink lemonade
  she slid down the straw and fell in."
  A limerick is five lines long, with a rhyme scheme. Lines 1, 2 and 5 have
  three feet, and lines 3 and 4 have two feet. The contest should be judged
  by all guests.
• Irish Yarn Game: Host starts Irish story. Characters and facts must be half
  true and half false. When host stops, they pick another guest to continue
  tale until last guest has completed Irish "yarn." Each guest then gets a
  chance to tell which parts they think were true and which were false.
  Discussion may last into the night.

226

April First Farces

Invitations

- Use a formal format and send three weeks in advance. Give a fictitious location for party, such as an exclusive restaurant or country club. When guests arrive at the restaurant, have a well-dressed person there to greet them and to present a list of clues so they can find the "real" party location.
- Have an emergency phone number on list so guests can call in case they never find party. List of clues should lead guests to a series of spots with a party representative at each (to keep them on track). Eventually, they should end up at host's home.

Prizes

Give a prize to the first guests and last guests to arrive. Prizes could be a gift certificate for a day of golf or dinner for two at the country club used on the invitation.

Menu

Serve an elegant sit-down dinner with champagne as a reward!

227

Easter at Golf Course

Invitations
- Have a picture of an Easter bunny playing golf.
- Hold an Easter "egg hunt" and hide colored golf balls around part of course. Get approval from golf course first.
- Return to home or club for brunch or luncheon.

Decorations
Put 6-12 golf balls into an egg carton. Cushion balls with colorful tissue paper or Easter grass. Decorate tops of cartons.

Games
Play round of golf using colored golf balls.

228

Women's Easter Hat Brunch

Invitations

- Purchase miniature straw hats at a craft center. Decorate hats with narrow ribbon and lace. Place invitation in crown of hat, and hand deliver to guests' homes.
- Invite friends to bring along a plain "Easter straw hat" to be decorated at the party and donated to a local hospital or nursing home. Can also be used as centerpieces.

Menu

Have a brunch featuring egg souffle, fruit salad, punch, mints, mixed nuts, jelly beans, and lamb-shaped cake.

Games

- Guests should decorate hats. Provide several types of material including satin, calico and checkered patterns, etc. Also have ribbons, lace, buttons, bows, silk flowers, feathers, and glue. Offer a prize for best-decorated hat. Have an "Easter hat" parade with background music.
- Pin the tail on the Easter Bunny. Make a large cotton tail and purchase large cardboard Easter bunny.

229

Let's Save Mother's Day

This party is best when given by Mother's immediate family.

- Forget the old routine of breakfast in bed, when "Mom" has to clean up. Instead, start the morning with a presentation of a fresh flower bouquet. Take her to her favorite breakfast/brunch restaurant (make advance reservations).
- After the meal, present Mother with "labor saving certificates" from all family members. These certificates state duties each family member will do for her. Out-of-towners can send certificates good for "promise to call, write, or visit."
  Sit back and watch Mother's face beam!
- Let her select a favorite movie or play she would like to attend that evening.

230

May Day Welcome Luncheon

Invitations
- Fill small May baskets with fresh flowers.
- Write the invitation on scroll-like paper; roll up and tie with colored ribbon.
- Place invitations in May basket.
- Hand deliver to new neighbors' homes.

Menu
- Do-it-yourself luncheon fare served buffet style.
- Have fruit juices of all types, pita-pocket bread, and an assortment of fillings such as egg, tuna, chicken salad, peanut butter, turkey, ham, beef, and various cheeses. Serve a vegetable platter with dips, fruit salad, and Jello salad.
- Dessert tray may include assorted cookies, candy bars, and ice cream sundaes.

Decorations
- Have party outdoors on a patio, deck, or garden, if available. Cover picnic tables with floral cloth (or paper) sheets.
- Place spring baskets with fresh flowers and ribbons around party area.

Games
Ask each guest to stand and tell the others about themselves, their family, hobbies, interests, etc.

231

Parade Party on the 4th of July

- Have a block party and parade for your entire neighborhood. Several weeks before the 4th of July, begin planning during a short meeting at your home. Delegate areas of the party and parade to volunteers, i.e., parade themes, games, invitations, decorations, food, etc.
- Children and adults can decorate bicycles, scooters, pets, wagons, and lawnmowers for the parade.

Games
- During the picnic, have one of the older children read a poem or a verse on independence of America.
- Organize a skit using the children. Many pre-written skits can be found in the library. (Practice before the party.)
- Have a pie-eating contest.
- Have a tug-of-war.
- Get a pig from a farm, grease it up, and try to catch it.

Menu
- Have a pot luck with several barbeque grills.
- Gather several ice cream makers and make homemade ice cream. Have toppings available.

232

Haunted House Party

For ages 13 to adult.

Invitations
Request guests to come disguised as their favorite Halloween character. Prizes can be given in various categories.

Decorations
- Use white bedsheets to cover all furniture and serving table. Decorate covered areas and walls with black yarn for cobweb effect. Continue to decorate entryway and rooms with store-bought cardboard skeletons, vampires, etc. Place candles of all sizes around the party area (if youngsters are invited, it is safer to use flashlights) for an unusual lighting effect. Carved pumpkins can be placed in windows.
- Set up a lighted area that can be used for photographing costumes. It is also fun to videotape the guests, and watch the videotape during the festivities.

Games
Charades: Divide guests into two or more teams. Before party, write charades to be performed. Select a team member to act charade chosen at random. Participant performs for his/her own team, within a designated time limit. The team with the most points wins.

233

Hobo Halloween Costume Party

Invitations
- Write on colored plates and glue patches of material on sides.
- Ask guests to dress as hobos with knapsacks.
- Invite a guest to bring a guitar for a sing-a-long.
- Hold party at a local park or backyard. Have a barrel with a fire inside it or a bonfire for warming hands and for roasting hot dogs and marshmallows.

Menu
Serve hot chocolate, tea, coffee, hot apple cider, hot dogs, marshmallows, and doughnuts.

Games
- Bob-for-Apples: Fill a large tub with water, and float apples.
- Pass-the-Orange: Divide guests into two teams. Each team passes one orange between members, but only using chins and necks. No hands allowed! The first team to pass orange through team wins. If orange is dropped, it must be brought back to the beginning again.

234

Thanksgiving Reunion Open House

Invitations
- Have party in late afternoon or early evening.
- Ask guests home from college to bring photos from college year.

Decorations
- Have a centerpiece of fresh fruit or flowers on buffet table.
- Use a Thanksgiving motif, and scatter fall leaves on tables. Also, hang store-bought cardboard turkeys on walls.
- Have a guest book at entrance to get everyone's new address. Make copies and give to guests as they leave.

Menu
A buffet featuring cold turkey salad, hot rolls, and a vegetable tray, and beverages such as hot apple cider and soft drinks. For dessert, serve pumpkin pie tarts with whipped cream, blonde brownies, nuts, and mints.

Games
Informal conversation and photograph-sharing will keep the guests busy.

235

"We Gather Together" Thanksgiving Day Party

Invitations
Choose a Thanksgiving symbol for front of invitation.

Decorations
- Use various sizes of gourds and cut a flat surface on each so it can stand.
- Cut a hole large enough for a candle to be placed in top.
- Set around room on tables.

Games
Cornucopia Memory Game: The starting player should name something to put in the cornucopia that begins with the letter "A," for example, "apple." The second player repeats "apple" and adds an object that begins with the letter "B." The game continues using the consecutive letters of the alphabet. This game is a fun way to test your memory and concentration!

Menu
- Harvest Soup: All guests are invited to bring one fresh vegetable to be added to a large pot of beef, tomato, or chicken stock. Guests are invited to prepare and add their contribution to the soup. Noodles or rice can also be added.
- Serve soup with turkey sandwiches and cranberry punch.
- For dessert, serve pumpkin or pecan pie with whipped cream, coffee, tea.

236

Day After Thanksgiving Shopper's Party

Invitations
- Invite female friends to the "biggest shopping day of the year!"
- Use a photocopy of a credit card or sales slip for the invitation.
- Invite guests to meet at a hostess's house for lunch and spend the afternoon shopping at your favorite stores for Christmas gifts.

Menu
No turkey! Serve chili, cornbread, cole slaw, and cherry cobbler pie with ice cream.

Games
- Shoppers' "Show and Tell": best bargain bought.
- Most purchases by one guest.
- Offer a store gift certificate for each winner.

Favors
Guests will create "personalized shopping bags" by decorating canvas bags with glitter, ribbon, and sequins. This can be done while waiting for everyone to arrive.

237

Christmas Eve Open House

A Christmas Eve Open House is a great occasion to share the holiday with friends, families, and relatives.

Invitations
- Choose a favorite Christmas symbol for cover of invitation.
- Invite guests to bring friends.
- Have party during afternoon or early evening.

Decorations
- Have ornaments available for guests to decorate Christmas tree.
- Christmas songs should be used as background music.

Menu
Offer hot cider, wassail punch, Christmas cookies and candies. Have cookie decorating table set up with sugar cookies, icing, and toppings.

Games
Plan to carol throughout neighborhood. Be prepared to have candles, flashlights, and song sheets.

238

"Up on the Housetop" Party for Children

Invitations
Make invitation out of Christmas sugar cookie; write the time and place with icing. Hand deliver cookie invitations to guests' homes.

Games
• Ask an adult to read "The Night Before Christmas" to children.
• Lead children in singing Christmas tunes.

Decorations
• Have a small-sized Christmas tree available for the children to decorate.
• Use baker's dough for children to shape into ornaments. Bake ornaments before placing on tree.
• Allow children to take ornaments home after party.

Menu
Have plates of peanut butter and jelly star-shaped sandwiches, carrot sticks, fruit juice, and Christmas cookies.

239

A Party for Every Season

Have guests come dressed according to a season of their choice. These costumes can range from bathing suits or ski outfits to a pretty spring dress and bonnet.

Menu

Serve foods that are appropriate to different times of year. The appetizer may consist of fruits and vegetables that are in season during the summer. For the main course, have a roasted turkey representing fall, etc. For dessert, try something that would be common during the winter or spring.

Activities

Have activities that are common for each season of the year. For example, a trivia game for winter, a beach ball for summer, apple bobbing for fall, and a softball game for spring.

240

January Calendar Party

Invitations
- The invitation should be written on a page (one month) from a calendar. Glue a colored piece of construction paper providing the information to the calendar page.
- Ask each person to dress appropriately for the month that they were sent.
- Guests should bring a gag present representing their month.

Activities
- Spider Web: Make a web of string by wrapping it around chairs, pictures, doorways, etc. (there should be one string for each guest). When guests arrive, have them follow one of the strings. At the end of each string, attach a prediction for the coming year. When everybody has one, they should read them aloud.
- Ten Years From Now: Have one person whisper to each guest the name of a place. Another should whisper the name of a person, and the third whispers an occupation. Each guest should create a scenario of what his or her life would be in ten years using these three clues.
- End evening by writing five New Year's resolutions.

Menu
Serve food combinations that include dates, for example, date nut sandwiches, date cake, and date nut bread. Make a clock out of deviled eggs and deli meat and cheeses.

241

Festival of Hearts

Invitations
- Invite guests with a valentine.
- Everyone should dress in red, pink, or white.

Games
- Have a progressive conversation, with each person taking a turn to speak for one minute on a subject dealing with love, for example, qualifications for a first date, their first kiss, most romantic memory, etc.
- Build a Love Nest: Divide into teams and have a contest to draw onto large pieces of paper the ideal love nest (this could be a whole house, a small cottage, or a room). Be creative! Set a timer, and allow each team three minutes to complete drawing.

Decorations
Hang large paper hearts on the walls and red, pink, and white streamers and balloons.

242

April Fool's Party

For teens and adults.

Invitations
Write the invitations backwards, so guests have to read them in a mirror.

Decorations
• Have colorful balloons taped to the floor.
• Hang posters upside-down.

Activities
• Fool's Course: Set up an obstacle course. Lead guests through the course so they know where obstacles are placed. Blindfold half the guests, remove the obstacles, and let the rest enjoy watching them stumble around nothing at all! Blindfold other half of guests and put obstacle course back quietly. Watch as guests try to remember "Fool's Course."
• Product Selling Contest: Each guest creates a silly product and promotes it. Audience votes which product they would buy, and the person with the most votes wins!
• Ask guests to tell the best practical joke that has happened to them in the past.

243

Spring Cleaning

Inspire your friends to clean their closets when spring has arrived.

Invitations
- Tell guests to dress in old clothes.
- Guests should bring trash bags filled with old clothes, shoes, toys, blankets, etc. that they want to give away to charity.

Activities
- Clothes Race: Divide into teams and fill baskets with a complete outfit. Have a relay race where each person must take a turn putting the clothes on, running to a certain point, returning to the next contestant, and passing the outfit on. The first team to have everyone go through the course wins.
- Have an expert available for makeovers and for choosing colors as a reward for the guests' charitable contributions.

244

Welcome Springtime!

For children 3-7 years.

Sometimes, winter lasts forever! Children certainly believe that it does.

Decorations
Hang large pieces of white construction paper on the walls and
let the children draw scenes of springtime with colorful crayons.

Activities
- Tell children to pretend they are seeds planted in the ground that are
  growing. The children must grow into flowers and then dance in the wind.
- Buy baskets and allow children to decorate them.
- Take the guests on a spring hike and tell them to find signs of spring such
  as newly budding flowers and nests filled with baby birds.
- Have the children collect loose nature items in their baskets which they will
  glue onto paper when they return to the party location. (If the party is near
  Easter, dye eggs and serve a bunny-shaped cake.)

245

Park Play

This is a great party to welcome spring for children 7 years and older. Host should bring a large softball for dodge ball, paper grocery bags, and string for a three-legged race.

Invitations
Write invitation on ripped paper bags and inform guests to wear old clothes.

Activities
- Dodge Ball: Divide into two groups. One group forms a circle and throws the ball to each other (only below the waist). The other group stands in the center and dodges the ball, trying not to get hit. As each person gets hit, they must join the circle. The last person left standing in the center is the winner.
- Three-Legged Race: Form teams of two. Each team is given a grocery sack and a piece of string. Each team member must put a leg into the grocery sack, tie the top, and run through a course.

246

Stars and Stripes

Guests are to come dressed in red, white, and blue. As each guest arrives, give him/her the song sheet of a patriotic song such as "America the Beautiful." After all the guests have arrived, tell the guests to hum the song they received. There will be two people singing each song and they must find each other! This is a good way for the guests to mingle and meet each other. Once the teams of two are formed, play a game of U.S. history trivia.

Activities
- Have guests write their own declaration of independence. For example, freedom from school, bills, alarm clocks, mothers-in-law, etc.
- Place a large cardboard star in the center of the room. Guests stand behind a line and try to throw bean bags onto star.
- Choose two guests to run against each other for "President of the Party"! Each candidate must give a speech telling what they will do for the party. Then have a secret ballot and choose the winner!

Menu
Serve fried chicken, apple pie, and cold salads.

247

Floating Picnic Auction

This is a great summertime party. Rent a party boat on a local river or lake. Hire a bluegrass band to perform on board. Invite several friends to co-host and share expenses.

Invitations
- Use a boat motif.
- Ask female guests to bring a decorated picnic box lunch for two.
- Male guests can bring beverages.

Activities
Auction the picnic box lunches (proceeds to go to a designated charity). The person with the highest bid will receive the lunch and the company of the chef.

Decorations
- Decorate the boat with balloons and streamers. Most rental boats have eating areas, kitchen facilities, and bathrooms.
- Have a talent show or a dance contest.

248

Summer Tree Party

This is a party for your friends who love the outdoors.

Invitations
• Meet at a local park or national forest.
• Guests should bring a picnic lunch and hiking boots.

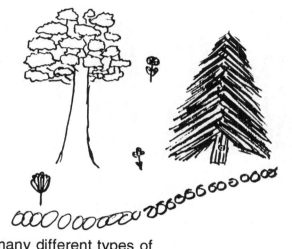

Activities
• Leaf Identification: Divide into teams and collect as many different types of leaves as possible. The most leaves with correct identification wins. (Bring a reference book to settle disputes.)
• Ask local nurseries to provide seedlings for the group to plant.
• Relax and enjoy the beauty of the forest.

249

School Days

This is a party for reminiscing about past school days.

Activities
- Nursery School: Place hunks of clay on a table. Everyone must make something to take home.
- Elementary School: Choose two captains to pick teams for a relay race.
- High School: The men run through a sports drill and the women learn a dance or a cheer.
- College: Everyone must read an article and discuss it.
- End the party with dancing to favorite old records!

Decorations
Place school books and pom-poms on tables. Hang diplomas and uniforms on walls.

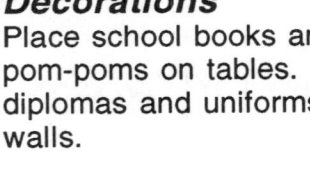

250

World Series Game Party

Invitations
- Cut paper into the shape of a baseball.
- Ask everyone to come wearing their favorite team's shirt or hat.
  Option: Invite guest to send money to host for a team party T-shirt.

Menu
Serve the same food found at a baseball park.

Games
- Divide guests into teams. Set up activities where teams can win points. The games should be determined by the interests and hobbies of the host and guests. The team with the most points at the conclusion of the party wins the "World Series" of games.
- Table tennis contest (2 of 3 wins).
- Jumping contest - longest and highest.
- Jump rope - longest.
- Softball pitch - try to hit cans from several distances.
- Hot dog eating contest - most or fastest.
- Best team cheer - most creative, most spirit.
- Tug of war.
- T-ball - farest hit.
For each game, pick number of players needed.
All team members must play once.

251

Autumn Leaves Party

This party is for children ages 3 and older.

Invitations
Tell the parents to dress the children warmly for playing outside.

Activities
- Fall is so beautiful. Organize outdoor activities such as raking leaves and jumping into the pile. Go on a hike and collect colorful leaves. Make a scarecrow with old clothes, straw, and leaves.
- If it is a windy day, see who can catch the most leaves as they fall from the trees. If the party is indoors, play pin the leaves on the trees (like pin the tail on the donkey). Bob for apples and let the children make their own caramel apples (under adult supervision).

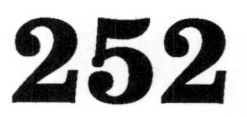

252

Spookie Special

Here's a party with a Halloween twist. Instead of coming in full costumes, the guests dress in regular clothes. The twist is everyone must wear hats and wigs.

Invitations
- Upon arrival paint guests' faces to look like scary creatures. Guests who have already been painted can paint arriving guests. Have hats available for those who come without costume.
- Give each guest paper and pen, turn off the lights, and tell everyone to draw something. Vote on best picture. You may do this a few times.
- String "Chewing" Contest: Inflate orange and black balloons and tie a piece of two-foot-long string to each. Each contestant must "eat" string until the balloon is next to mouth. May be done in teams.

253

Silver Moon Frolic

For teens and adults (couples and singles).
This party must be held in the fall near Halloween or Thanksgiving.

Invitations
Cut black construction paper into moon shapes and glue onto gold or silver paper. Fold card style, and write party information inside.

Decorations
- Decorate the party area with suspended crescent moons made of silver and gold foil (hang with nylon fishing line). Hang silver and gold tinsel from ceiling. Stars can also be hung.
- Set up a telescope on a patio or by a window for "moon gazing."
- Play music that has a moon theme, and dance under the stars!

Menu
Moon soup (matzoh ball soup) consisting of chicken and dumplings with moon biscuits. Serve orange Jello salad in round shapes with cream cheese frosting.

254

Pumpkin Carving for Couples

For adults.

Invitations
- Invite all your friends to your home to carve pumpkins.
- Tell guests to bring their own pumpkins and carving tools.

Menu
Serve roast beef sandwiches with homemade bread, salads, and apple chunks covered with melted caramel for dessert.

Activities
- Have guests carve the pumpkins in the likeness of their mate. An award will be given to the pumpkin that most resembles the person.
- Bob for apples and play charades.

255

Pilgrim Party

Re-enact the first Thanksgiving!

Invitations
- Tell guests to bring a dish that the Pilgrims might have eaten.
- Guests should wear Pilgrim clothes and hats.
- Have the party outdoors on long picnic tables.

Activities
- Have a campfire.
- Let the guests tell what they envision the experience of the Pilgrims to have been like.
- Organize guests to form a circle. The first person should invent a few Pilgrim-like steps. The next person repeats these steps and adds his or her own. This should continue around circle until dance is complete. Then, everyone should do the whole dance together.

256

Lip Sync Festival

Invitations
Invite at least 20 people over for a night of "caroling." Don't tell them they will be lip syncing.

Activities
Upon arrival have guests pick a favorite Christmas song. Pick a partner and rehearse the performance. The host can make the whole thing more fun by playing male recording artists when the women lip-sync. Judge by having all guests give a score of 1-10 based on delivery, creativity, and acting ability.

257

Winter Wonderland

Many people spend winter wondering when it will be over! Break the winter chill by planning a beach party.

Invitations

Tell guests to come dressed in summer wear (make sure house is warm!).

Menu

Have a barbeque with hamburgers, hot dogs, chicken, fruit, and vegetable salads.

Decorations

Hang paper palm trees, posters of Hawaii, bathing beach beauties, and bodybuilders.

Activities

- Divide into teams. You will need four inner tubes, two snorkels, and several bananas. Two team members squeeze into an inner tube and run to a banana. They must peel and eat the banana using only one hand each. Then, they must pick up the snorkel between their knees, and pass it to the next two waiting in line.
- Divide into couples and give each a glass of water. The couples must dance a fast song while holding the glass. The winners are the ones who have the most water left in their glass.
- Play old surfer videos on the television.

258

Holiday Gag Gift

Invitations
- Invite friends over for a pre-Christmas caroling and gift exchange.
- Tell guests to bring a gag gift.

Menu
Serve Christmas goodies and complement with cider, tea, and hot chocolate.

Activities
- Put gag gifts into a pile and give each guest a number. Then in numerical order, choose gifts one by one. As each person chooses a gift, he or she is able to exchange it with any of the gifts that were previously chosen. Hopefully your friends are not overly polite, because stealing each other's gifts is the fun part!
- Print song sheets and hire a musician or sing a cappella.

259

Movie Magic

For all ages.

Winter can be a cold and long season. Break up a winter week by inviting friends over to enjoy a movie together.

Menu
Serve hot chocolate, hot apple cider, buttered popcorn, and bowls of movie candy.

Activities
Add to the excitement by showing something that everyone has not yet seen, for example, a retrospect, documentary, or new release. Review the movie afterwards!

260

Progressive Pool Party

This can be an adults only or a children included party and is great for a hot summer day. It takes careful planning with neighbors and friends who have backyard pools. Ask each to host a particular time of day and provide snacks or menu to coordinate with other hosts.

Once you have sent the invitations and selected the menus, all that is left is to pack your bathing suits, shorts, towels, sunblock, and enjoy!

Menu
A simple menu works best. Cut expenses by having guests bring their own beverages.

Activities
Pool Games: pool volleyball, water ballet, pool tag, and Marco Polo.

261

Grammy Award Party

This is a great party for music buffs and should be held while the awards are airing on television. Region: Southern California

Invitations
• Have a picture of the Grammy award on the front.
• Ask each guest to bring Grammy nominated songs/records to be played during party.

Activities
• When guests arrive, provide pencils and a list of all nominations, and let the voting begin!
• Turn on T.V. and chart the results on a large tally board.
• Offer a prize for the guest who guesses the most winners
  (perhaps a certificate to a record store).

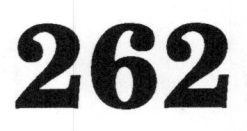

262

Last Fling in the Summer Cabin Party

Region: Cape Cod

- The perfect solution to all the melancholy felt at the end of a wonderful summer. Invite all the friends and neighbors over to help clear out the refrigerator and make a large pot of soup or spaghetti using up all the leftovers from the kitchen.
- This is a good impromptu party. If you invite family members, you may even get some help with the "boat and dock out of the water" projects and the storing of lawn items, etc.
- Reward faithful helpers with a moonlight boat cruise with soft music and champagne on board.
- Last, but not least, let everyone tell their "favorite" tale of the summer, either past or present.

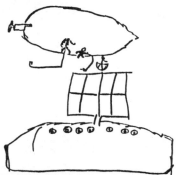

263

Colorado Gold Panning Party

Invitations
Invite guests to join you in costume as "Pan Gold Miners."

Decorations
Host party at a park with a creek area. Check with park authorities to reserve an area beside creek. Paint or spray pebbles gold before party and place in creek for guests to find.

Menu
Make "barrel lunches" for guests (one for each couple). Put cold chicken and the fixings in a plastic bucket, and provide beverages.

Activities
Offer a prize for the "miner who pans the most gold."

264

Going to the Dogs

A racetrack outing in Florida.

• This party can be an actual outing to the local dog track or can feature a dog race on cable television. If you go to a track, choose an afternoon when the crowd is not as large.
• Set up the party area with "betting windows" and copy race forms from the newspaper to distribute to your guests. Many stores in Florida offer decorations with the racing motif. You may wish to find posters of the dogs and track to enhance the setting. Use play money for betting. Use a large chalkboard to post winners.

Menu
Hot dogs, Polish dogs, sauerkraut dogs, cheese dogs, beverages, and ice cream.

265

Georgia Peach Luncheon Dance

Instead of a dinner/dance, try a weekend peach luncheon dance!
Best held in Spring or Summer, outside on patio or garden area.

Decorations
Fresh flowers with peaches in arrangements. Set up a long,
elegant buffet table in adjoining room to dance area.

Menu
Chicken salad, fresh fruit salad with pecan roll, peach melba,
peach cobbler, peach mimosas, etc.

Activities
Live music is best, but there is great dance music on records and tapes.
Select appropriate music according to age and taste of guests who are invited.

266

Indiana Hoosier Skip-Bo Card Party

"Skip-Bo" is a popular card game played all around the Hoosier state, especially during the wintertime.

Invitations
- Use the Skip-bo cards as invitations with party information printed on back of cards.
- Invite 6-18 guests (a set of Skip-bo cards will be needed for a game of 6 players).
- Dress should be casual and comfortable.

Decorations
- Decorate party area with all types of playing cards and hang enlarged posters of card's names on walls.
- Have a set number of card tables, and place rules of game and deck of cards on each table.

Menu
Sloppy joes, sub sandwiches, chips, dip, beer, and sodas.

267

Sand & Sun Volleyball Party

Invitations
- Go California style. Call your friends a few days in advance and invite them to a local park or beach to play volleyball.
- Ask guests to each bring one thing that makes them think of California to decorate party area.

Activities
- Set up teams and have a tournament.
- Make sure to have good music available to play to.
- Don't forget the sunscreen.

Menu
Bring lots of liquid and portable snacks. Nothing elaborate.

268

A Windy Day in Kansas Kite Party

Invitations
- Make invitations in the shape of kites with yarn or ribbons. Print party information on front.
- Invite guests to come and make their own creation for flying.

Decorations
Have tables set up for kite-making with craft materials. Set a time limit on making the kites. Guests can form teams for creating kites (offer prizes for best kite).

Menu
Outdoor buffet with cold salads and sandwiches, cool lemonade and juices.

Activities
Kite flying contests (highest, most acrobatic, fastest, etc.).

269

Kentucky Derby Party

For all ages. This party requires advance planning and plenty of television sets.

Invitations
Anything having to do with horses, perhaps paper horseshoes with information printed around shape.

Decorations
• Print copies of race sheets and pass out at door. Have chips available for betting.
• Hang balloons and enlarged copies of race sheet.
• Be certain to videotape race so it can be played over again (offer prizes for guests who picked winners).

Menu
Serve mint juleps and finger sandwiches during race. After race is over, a heartier meal or small cakes and cookies may be served.

270

Eastern Shore Clambake

Invitations
- Clam shell picture with information inside clam.
- Dress should be casual. Tell guests to bring bathing suits.

Decorations
Build a large bonfire on beach.

Menu
Dig pits for clams and potatoes. Cook s'mores over fire, and fill a washtub with ice and beverages.

Activities
- Ask guests to bring musical instruments.
- Eat, drink, tell stories, and sing the night away.

271

Minnesota Winter Wonderland

Invitations
- Snowflake-shaped lace glued to front of card. Glue snow and glitter on front.
- Tell guests to dress warmly and bring skates, cross-country skis, hockey equipment, etc.
- Party area is best by lake with a warm house nearby.

Activities
- Purchase blocks of ice and have an ice sculpture contest (tell guests to plan a design beforehand). Guests may form teams.
- Ice skating, skiing, ice hockey, etc.

Menu
Serve hot toddies, hot chocolate, and cider. Offer a huge pot of chicken or beef stew with freshly baked bread. For dessert, serve warm apple pie.

272

Wall Street Welcome

Invitations
- Photocopy a stock report. Glue party information inside.
- Dress should be pin-striped business suits and ties, and briefcases.

Activities
- Stocks and bonds trivia game.
- Pin names of famous corporate executives on backs of guests. Guests must ask questions to find out who "they are."
- Prizes may be subscriptions to a financial magazine.

Decorations
- Decorate party area with stock papers from newspapers and magazines.
- Put hors d'oeuvres on a desk.
- Have real and fake telephones all around the room.

Menu
Deli-type bag lunches and large kosher pickles, potato chips, and soft pretzels.

273

Oklahoma Country Rock Hoedown

Ages 13 to 100 years.

Invitations
- Hold party in a large room (may be public or private).
- Dress should be in country style jeans, boots or comfortable shoes.

Decorations
- Decorate party room with bales of hay, posters of rodeo and country scenes.
- Party favors could be multi-colored bandanas.

Menu
Simple buffet fare featuring sloppy joes, chips, baked beans, brownies, etc.

Activities
Have a square dance. Find a professional to demonstrate and teach guests how to dance. Call local country radio station and ask if a "local celebrity" might be able to attend.

274

San Francisco Opera-at-Home Party

This is a good idea for couples with small children at home.

Invitations
- Use an opera theme for invitations.
- Tell guests to bring their favorite opera recorded for listening.
- Dress should be formal, with tuxedos and gowns.

Decorations
Have candlelight and fresh flowers.

Menu
Select menus from books for entertaining available at your library.
Sample menu might be: Melon, Paupiettes of Sole, Potatoes Persillés, Petits Pois Grandmère, Apricot and Pineapple Flan with Almonds.
Sounds tough, but research recipes that can be prepared in advance and allow you to enjoy your own party.

Activities
Rent a video of a well-known opera or have guests talk about their favorite performance.

275

Grand Ol' Opry Presents

This is a country western music awards party.

Invitations
• Use a photocopy of the Grand Ol' Opry for the invitation.
• Host party on evening of music awards show.
• Copy a list of nominees and present a list to each guest for choosing winners.

Decorations
Hang posters of Nashville and country western stars.

Menu
Pitchers of beer, sausages, gravy and biscuits with grits. Make homemade ice cream!

Activities
Turn on television set and join the celebration. Play country western records.

276

Vail Ski Tea

There are always parties after a long day of skiing in Vail, Colorado! How about a high tea to change the pace!

Menu
• Hot soup with cucumber sandwiches, English muffins, crackers, jelly, soft cheeses, cookies, Sacher torte with herbal teas, and lemonade.
• Serve food on small tables by fire; use throw pillows instead of chairs.

Decorations
Decorate party area with spring-like potted plants, tulips, daffodils, etc. Have a fire roaring to warm up the guests!

Activities
Enjoy the fire, conversation, and good friends.

277

To the Hounds Hunt Breakfast

During the months of November through March, the Virginia countryside is popular fox hunt territory. There is always a traditional hunt breakfast, or luncheon following a hunt.

Activities
- Have your own "mock hunt" event by dressing in hunt attire and discussing fox hunt folklore and traditions.
- Play "To the Hounds" hunt background music.
- Contact local horse facilities to check if they have hunts to watch or ride in.

Menu
Offer drinks with a buffet featuring Virginia baked ham, biscuits, gravy, salad, and crab cakes. Irish coffees are great to have for dessert.

278

State of the Union Address

Invitations
- Use pictures of state flowers, birds, or flags folded in half with information inside.
- Guests should dress in costume of their state of birth, and have their state history, flower, bird, motto, flag, etc. on a piece of paper.

Menu
Call guests in advance and ask for their favorite "down home" dishes. Incorporate these recipes into a varied menu. Serve buffet style with multi-colored plates and napkins.

Decorations
Balloons, streamers, state travel posters, and centerpieces with state flags.

Activities
- Research specific games played in certain areas of the country.
- Offer a prize for the best presentation of state, best costume, etc.

279

Disaster Party

Disasters such as earthquakes, tornados, hurricanes, floods, or snowstorms happen all over the country. Why not share with your friends and neighbors a party to lift everyone's spirit. If appropriate, ask everyone to bring old bedding, clothes, toys, etc. to be given to families who may have lost homes.

Activities
• Let everyone tell what they were doing when the disaster occurred.
• Play a game that everyone can participate in, such as trivia games, charades, etc.

Menu
Ask everyone to bring a dish to share buffet style.

280

Nebraska Corn Roast

A great casual picnic party outdoors.

Invitations
Corn motif, of course. Ask guests to wear jeans and work shirts, and give checkered neck scarves as favors.

Decorations
Old corn husks from the fields, checkered tablecloths, and sunflower centerpieces on serving tables.

Activities
Game of flag football. Use neck scarf in pockets as flags.

Menu
- Roast corn in husks over charcoal grill (soak corn in husk 2-3 hours in cold salt water before grilling) 20 minutes on front and back of corncob. Serve corn by pulling husks back and dipping corncob in melted butter kept in two-pound coffee cans sitting on grill to keep hot.
- Grilled hamburgers or steak with baked potatoes and baked beans.

281

Cross-Country Ski Outing

Invitations
Invite your guests to bundle up, bring their cross-country skis, and join you on your favorite ski trails around a lake or State park.

Activities
Meet at park. Give guests ski trail maps with return time and place. After dinner, exchange ski "war stories."

Menu
- Light fireplace and set buffet table near fire.
- Arrange seating about fireplace.
- Serve a hearty supper of hot Swedish beef stew, hot yeast rolls, hot toddies, hot chocolate, and Swedish coffee. Cheese and fruit to finish.

282

Tastes of the Globe

Birthday party for food lovers.

Invitations
- Copy a picture of the globe on the front of a folded card. Write information inside.
- Select four or five countries and ask guests to choose one and dress accordingly.
- Ask guests to bring a story (either folklore or humorous) about their country to tell aloud.

Activities
- Play background music representing each country.
- World Trivia: Pick teams and have each team randomly select a trivia question about the theme countries (before party, write trivia questions on slips of paper). Travel trivia games can be purchased at toy or game store. The team with the most points wins the contest. Award prizes that are travel related.

Menu
- Select ethnic dishes from each of the countries you have chosen for your theme.
- Set a buffet table for each country selected. Decorate with country's flag and other decorations representing the culture (you will save time if you purchase prepared food from ethnic restaurants).

283

Arabian Nights with Genie

Decorations
- Greet your guests in Arabian costume (with your "hunk" of a bodyguard in costume also).
- Remove all furniture. Set up a walk-in lightweight tent and decorate with curtains.
- Light perfumed incense candles for an added mystical touch.
- Scatter large pillows on floor. Arrange low tables and use for serving Arabian cuisine.

Activities
- Enlist a helper to be your "snake charmer."
- Hire a professional belly dancer to perform and teach guests the basics.

Kangaroos, Koalas, and Platypuses

This "down under" Australian hiking party needs to be held at a park or farm area (preferably near water). Reserve a space in advance.

Invitations
• Attach or draw pictures of kangaroos, koalas, or platypuses on front of folded card.
• Meet at host or hostess's house for a hearty breakfast.
• Separate into groups for a "scavenger hike."
• Recommend that guests dress casually and wear hiking boots.

Decorations
• Decorate party room with Australian travel posters (found at travel agencies).
• Place stuffed kangaroos, koalas, and platypuses on tables.
• For a party favor, give gold stickpins for guests to wear on lapels.

Activities
• Pass out maps and clues and carpool to park.
• Set a time limit and arrange a place to meet after hunt.
• Scavenger Hunt.
• Greet returning hikers with a pot of fresh Australian coffee and lamb stew over a campfire.

285

Brazilian Birthday Party for the Fami

Invitations
- Invitations are traditionally telephoned, not written.
- Include children and parents.

Decorations
- Brazilian birthdays are very festive and colorful. Use plenty of colorful balloons and streamers.
- Arrange several tables (one for displaying the cake).

Menu
- Set one table with hors d'oeuvres.
- Serve bomba (French éclairs), Napoleans, sweets, fruits, and jellies.

286

Inuit and Northwest Native Art Outing

This party will appeal to guests who are interested in Inuit native art and history. Make arrangements with several galleries in advance for a visit. Another style of art may be substituted.

Activities
- Proceed by carpool to a local library or gallery where you can arrange a video presentation and a speaker on Inuit art and customs.
- Have a tour guide available to walk group through the gallery.
- After dinner, play "Twenty Questions" on Inuit art and customs. The winner should be awarded with a piece of artwork or a book on Inuit art which can be purchased at a gallery or museum.

Menu
- Begin outing with beverages and canapés.
- Upon return home, serve a simple dinner with wine.

287

Chinatown Challenge

Enlist the help of several friends who have vans.

Invitations
- Use the red gate of China theme on front of card.
- Invite female friends to join you for a luncheon, shopping, and tour of your local Chinatown area.
- Meet at hostess's home.

Decorations
Decorate interior of vans with Chinese decor.

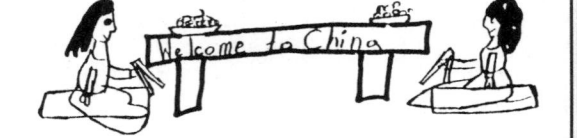

Activities
- Give a net-type shopping bag with a personalized name tag as a favor to each guest as they arrive at your home for holding their treasures.
- Head for shopping street and have fun searching for the many bargains available.
- Make advance reservations at a Dim Sum or typical Chinese restaurant in Chinatown. Dim Sum is a variety of foods in small servings brought to tables on a trolley cart. This is good for tasting and sharing.
- After meal, relax with Chinese tea, and show and tell your shopping bargains!
- Explain China's oldest game, "Go." Description found at library.

288

Birthday English-Style

This party is for children.

Decorations
• Hang balloons, streamers, and birthday cards on walls.
• Set the table with colorful plates, napkins, and party hats.

Activities
• Sardines: One child hides while the other guests look for him or her. The child who finds him or her must hide too! Continue searching until all children are hiding together. It is fun squeezing together like sardines if the space is too small!
• Musical Bumps: This is similar to musical chairs except the players may sit anywhere. The last one to sit is out. A judge is needed for this game.

Menu
• Serve egg, ham, or tomato sandwiches, hot cross buns, gelatin desserts, fruit salad, and cookies.
• Bake a fortune cake! Mix small charms into the batter before baking. A ring signifies marriage; a thimble means you will be an old maid or bachelor.
• Make sure to boil charms and rings before adding to batter. Be careful when you bite.

289

Globe Theatre Revisited Party

Recreate your own Elizabethan "Globe Theatre" with painted or rented sets and enlarged photos from history books.

Invitations
Invite guests to come costumed as their favorite Shakespearean character with a monologue to recite.

Menu
Serve a heavy buffet featuring English shepherd's pie or leg of lamb with trimmings. During recitals, offer a dessert of plum pudding with assorted teas and sherry.

290

Fish and Chips Party

Invitations
Create invitation in shape of fish with the British flag on it.

Decorations
- Decorate party to resemble a British pub. Have a bar with stools.
- Research authentic British pubs at the library.
- Play British music.

Activities
- Paper Bag Dramatics: Give one lunch-sized paper bag filled with small items for props (such as a toothbrush, stamp, pencil, pen) to each guest. Ten minutes will be given to create a skit using the British pub theme.
- Darts: This game originated in England and is played in all the local pubs.

Menu
Serve fish (white bait fritters) and chips in newspaper, and have plenty of vinegar to season.

fish on plate

291

Cannes at Home Film Festival

Have your "own" Cannes foreign film festival! This is a great party for all movie buffs. Enlist the help of your local video stores to rent current popular foreign films. Rent several videos and borrow or rent two or three VCRs and televisions. Feature different "film screenings" in separate rooms.

Invitations
• Request guests to "dress the part" of stars and movie moguls.
• As guests enter party, give each a pair of glittered sunglasses as a party favor.

Decorations
Hollywood it up! Use glitter and glitz everywhere. Hang movie posters and enlarged maps on walls.

292

This is My Country

Invitations
Use a flag, or a cut-out in the shape of a country, for the cover of the invitation. Write party information on back. Ask for R.S.V.P. and notice of which country each guest will be representing. Ask guests to wear costumes from the country of their ethnic background. They should come prepared to talk about "the history of my country," celebrities from their country, famous dishes, etc.

Decorations
Go to the library to research decoration ideas. Perhaps you can discover a famous artist from each country. Find flowers and balloons in country's colors, etc.

Activities
- Research specific games played in different countries. The library offers many books on this subject. Do not hesitate to use children's games if necessary!
- A parade of the countries is a must. Have each guest present his or her country.
- Offer prizes from different countries' themes.

Menu
Check with library for ethnic recipe books. Have a varied and flavorable buffet style menu. Serve cocktails that are popular in different countries.

293

La Quartorze Celebration

In France, July 14 is independence day. So, join Parisians with costumes, music, dancing, and even your own parade to celebrate the anniversary of the French revolution.

Invitations
- Use "Les Miserables" as your theme for invitations or just a French flag design.
- Ask guests to dress in costume from the French Revolution (or in just red, white, and blue).

Activities
Cricket should be played if weather permits.

Menu
Offer a wide choice of wines, bread, and cheeses.
Top off with French pastries and Espresso.

294

Gemutlichkeit Birthday Party

This party has a German theme and is for all ages.

Invitations
Ask guests to dress in German costumes and to bring gifts fitting for the theme.
Or, host and hostess may greet guests in costume.

Decorations
- Decorate the party room with beer steins, and use a cuckoo clock decorated with fresh flowers for the centerpiece.
- Hang maps of Germany on the walls.

Activities
- Hire a good Polka band (or play Polka records). Polka the night away!
- The evening would not be complete without singing German favorites. Pre-arrange a lead singer and have song sheets available for guests to follow.

295

Israel Birthday Tradition

Invitations
- Invite all classmates, friends, and family members personally.
- In recreating an Israeli party, there should not be a time limit and there should be a lot of guests!

Activities
- If your party is for a small child, place him or her in a chair and have their father or uncle raise them up in the air as many times as they are old. This is for good luck!
- The birthday child should wear a wreath of fresh flowers made by their mother or grandmother.
- Israelis sing many songs to honor the birthday person.
- Go to the library to research Israeli games.

Menu
- Serve a buffet-style meal and be sure to have an abundance of food including candies, nuts, raisins, and cakes.
- Allow the children to sit on floor to eat and play games.

296

Fiesta Americana Style

Decorations
Decorate party area with large, colorful paper flowers and crepe paper.
Hang posters of bullfights, serapes, Mexican hats, and
musical instruments.

Activities
• Fill a piñata with candy and favors and hang it in an open area. Blindfold
  guests and give each a chance to break open the piñata with a stick.
  Everybody is a winner!
  (There is a religious significance in some areas. The piñata represents the
  devil tempting mankind with sweets. The blindfolded guest represents
  Christian faith.)
• Teach the Mexican hat dance and other folk dances.
• Play Mexican background music or have a live band.

Menu
Have a make-your-own taco bar complete with enchiladas, arroz con
pollo (chicken, rice, and tomato sauce), tostada salad, and margaritas.
Flan (egg custard) for dessert.

297

Sushi Surprise

Invitations
- Cut out the shape of a fish from Japanese rice paper. Write party information on reverse.
- Guests should wear costumes representing the history of a Japanese province.
- Guests need to remove shoes upon entering party.

Decorations
Hang travel posters and make Japanese screens with
lightweight paper.

Activities
- Origami Demonstration: Call an art department at a local
  college for references.
- Play Japanese background music.
- Shogi: Play this Japanese chess game.

Menu
Serve saki and sushi and follow with a traditional Japanese meal including
tempura and rice. Eat with chopsticks.

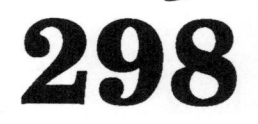

298

White Nights in Leningrad

White nights begin June 22, when it is light 24 hours a day.

Invitations
• Host party during daytime or use spotlights and extra lighting to brighten party area.
• Ask each guest to come with three interesting facts about Russia to be used in trivia game.

Decorations
• Decorate rooms with Bolshoi Ballet and Russian travel posters or copies of Russian art and artifacts.
• Borrow videotapes of Swan Lake Ballet.

Activities
• Play Russian trivia game and give Matryoshka dolls.
• Play Tchaikovsky for background music.

Menu
Begin with smoked salmon and champagne or famous Russian caviar and chilled Stolichnaya vodka. Serve Borscht red cabbage soup and hard bread rolls.

299

Global Wine and Cheese Tasting Fete

Invitations
- Invite your guests to join you at the "club" or social room for a global wine and cheese fete.
- Assign each guest or couple to bring wine and cheese from a specific region or country (suggest Gouda, Havarti, Fontina, Muenster, Greek Feta, Bleu Cheese, Provolone, etc. and wines from Italy, Germany, France, the United States, Spain, etc.). Guests should inform you of the country of their choice.

Decorations
- Hang posters, flags, and streamers representing all countries.
- Place small flags in stands by each country's wine and cheese display.
- Use color-coordinated paper products.

Activities
Ask a local wineshop and cheese store to recommend an authority to oversee your wine-tasting.

300

Swedish Daisy Crowns Picnic

Since summer is such a short season in Sweden, many Swedes like to picnic as often as weather permits.

Invitations
Ask guests to bring bunches of daisies. You should provide lightweight floral wire.

Activities
• Invite a guitarist to play Swedish folk music.
• Make Daisy Crowns: Create floral head wreaths with flowers and wire. You can also braid three daisy stems together for a daisy chain for bracelets and necklaces.

Menu
• Prepare a picnic meal in clever container for couples to share. Set table with a large checkered tablecloth or sit on the grass.
• Serve wine and cheese.

301

Swedish Christmas Dinner

Invitations
Ask guests to dress in formal attire.

Decorations
- Place a basket at front door and fill with Swedish postcards of the King and Queen of Sweden (write the names of the male guests on the King postcards). Have each female guest choose one card for a random selection of dinner partners.
- Set a long harvest table with a red cloth, white candelabra, and dozens of white votive candles in glass goblets. Place split logs on tables and surround with spruce branches.

Activities
- Children, dressed in long white robes (girls with silver tinsel headbands and boys with tall white hats) should carol during dessert. Each child should carry a white, lit candle. At end of caroling, someone dressed as St. Lucia should appear with a wreath of five candles on her head.
- Have two adults in traditional Swedish costume to do a Swedish folk dance.

Menu
Serve a Swedish smorgasbord complete with red caviar, smoked reindeer meat, a crisp glazed suckling pig with an apple in its mouth, hot sweet 'n sour cabbage, and a Swedish dessert.

302

Top of the World Pakistan Tea

This is a tea with the Mir who is one of the last Rajas! Convert
your party area into Shangri-La as recounted in *Lost Horizon*
by James Hilton.

Invitations
Ask guests to dress in ethnic costumes.

Decorations
• Enlarge a map of Pakistan and hang it on the wall
  along with posters of the Nagai Himalayas.
• Play ethnic background music.

Activities
• Have your own Raja to expound myths of the local area.
• Play traditional Pakistani games such as the "Old Lady, Old Lady"
  catching game (check your local library for rules).

Menu
Serve tea and Pakistan cakes and sweets.

303

French Birthday Party

Invitations
- In following the French tradition, your party will be very casual. Invitations should be extended personally to close friends of the family.
- Hold party at 4:00 pm during the usual afternoon snack time.

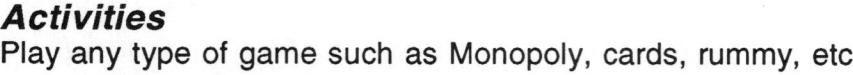

Activities
Play any type of game such as Monopoly, cards, rummy, etc.

Menu
Since you will not need special decorations for this party, save your efforts for baking or buying a fancy tiered birthday cake! In addition, serve sandwiches cut into fancy shapes, pastries, and petits fours.

304

Dating Game

This is a great singles party theme. Invite a few friends to help you plan the party. Do not invite too many guests who already know each other. Send each guest a questionnaire (covering hobbies, goals, etc.) which should be sent back before the party begins. Match the guests as best you can. Serve appetizers and let the guests mingle.

Activities
Start the show! Have the men stand on one side of the room and the women on the other. Read a brief description of each guest, then read the matched couples names. When everybody has been matched, it's date time. Couples can go on their date alone or in groups!

305

Directors and Stars

This party takes some effort by guests, but the result is well worth it.

Invitations
- Send an invitation to couples for a film festival. The catch is, they have to make their own film!
- Guests should rent or borrow video cameras and make a film before the party. The film can be anything: a home movie, a documentary, or simple scenery.

Activities
- As the party begins, ask guests to wear sunglasses and look and act like movie stars.
- After visiting a while, sit down and view the films together. Everyone should vote afterwards for the "best comedy," "best actor," etc.

Menu
Serve a lavish dessert buffet to celebrate all the hard work and good laughs!

306

Critic's Choice

Invitations
- Everyone enjoys watching movies. Send an invitation to all your friends to meet at a theatre to view a current movie.
- Everyone should come to your house afterward for coffee and desserts.
- Review the movie together or play your favorite movie trivia game.

307

Funniest Home Videos

Everyone likes watching videos and what is funnier than seeing friends taking their first bath as a one year old or falling off a ladder at 30 years! Make sure everyone knows there is a five minute maximum time limit. Set the scene by borrowing or renting director's chairs.

Invitations
• Cut out a cardboard star and glue glitter on front. Write party information on reverse.
• Ask guests to wear sunglasses and look "starish."

Menu
Serve popcorn, candy, and other movie theatre goods.

308

Purely Political

Come as your favorite political statement! Each guest gets five to ten minutes (depending on how many guests) to speak his or her mind. The host should ring a bell when the time runs out. This party can be educational and humorous. There should not be any debating or interruptions. After the speaking, let guests mingle; most guests will gravitate towards someone they want to hear more from.

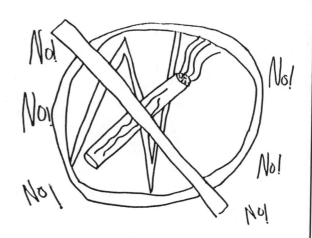

Menu
Serve appetizers and beverages.

309

Cowboys Kick Up

Invitations
Everyone must come dressed in western attire.

Decorations
- Decorate party area with wagon wheels, bales of straw, and scarecrows that resemble cowboys. For a real country touch, try to borrow some live chickens.
- Cover tables with red-and-white checkered tablecloths and empty wine bottles holding candles as the centerpieces.

Activities
- Hire a square dance caller and have a square dance.
- After dancing, take guests on a hayride.

Menu
Serve ranch beans, barbequed beef in buns, corn on the cob, and make-your-own sundaes.

310

Save The Earth Effort

This party is for all of your gardener friends and those who just want to give us a healthier environment.

Invitations
- Cut out the shape of a tree with green cardboard. Write party information on front. Ask each family to bring a healthy young tree to plant in a local park.
- Secure a state or local permit before party.

Menu
Prepare picnic lunches or an early supper to serve in the park after planting trees.

311

Sadie Hawkin's Party

Do you remember the Sadie Hawkin's dance when you were in high school? This party is the chance for ladies to bring the man of their choice! Also, this is a great singles party if you have many unmatched friends!

Invitations
- Address all invitations to females only.
- Each female should bring two box lunches which will be auctioned off.

Activities
- Man Hunt: All women are blindfolded and placed in the middle of a circle formed by the men. As the game begins, the women try to catch a man while the men rotate the circle around and around.
- A couple should hold an apple in place between their foreheads while they attempt to dance. At the end of the song, the couple with the apple still in place receives a prize.
- Auction off box lunches. Men bid on lunches and dine with the female who prepared it.

Decorations
- Decorate the party area with a country theme.
- Play old mountain music.

312

Alter Ego Party

Welcome to fantasyland! Everyone must come dressed as someone or something they have always wanted to be. Decorate the party area with pillows and balloons to resemble heavenly clouds.

Activities

Story Scramble: Each guest starts a story about the dream person whom they resemble in a 30 second time limit. Then, the other guests are given 30 seconds to add to the story. Let every guest have a chance to tell their story.

Menu

Serve dream puffs and other desserts with coffee, tea, and hot chocolate.

313

Mystery Fifties Party

Dress in fifties dress, for example, saddle shoes, poodle shirts...the works! Invitation will give clues for guests to go to "local" fifties type places (drive-in movie theatre, record shop, diner, etc.). At each destination the guests will discover another clue to help them "figure out" where the fifties party is located! The first guest or couple to find party will win a prize. The party location may be your home, bowling alley, roller skating rink, etc.

Decorations
• Hang balloons, crepe paper, streamers, fifties movie stars' posters.
• Party favors might be sunglasses, 45 rpm records.

Activities
Have a sock hop and dance to fifties music.

Menu
Serve a simple meal of sloppy joes, chips, French fries, cherry and chocolate cola.

314

Husbands as Servants

This is a party for the men to plan. The objective is to give wives a chance to be "princesses." The men should be real gentlemen and should not swear or tell sports stories!

Activities
List 10 activities such as a foot massage, a poem recital, a dance, a walk in a garden, etc. All of the men have duplicate lists. Each man allows his wife to order what she wants by giving him a number. The man looks at the number, then performs the activity.

Menu
The men make and serve a meal (can be a barbeque). The women will love the idea of not cooking!

315

All Night Slumber Party

Invitations
- This is a party "by the light of the moon."
- Cut out moon shapes for invitations.
- Ask guests to bring their sleeping bags, tents, flashlights, pajamas, and a favorite ghost story!

Decorations
Set up your backyard to resemble a campground with a campfire. Have the party begin around eight o'clock, so you won't have to serve dinner.

Activities
Go on a night hike. If you don't live in the country, drive to the nearest walking path. Return and take turns telling ghost stories.

Menu
Serve fruit salad, Danishes, juice, and coffee for breakfast.

316

Comic Caper

This party is pure fun and games.

Invitations
- Ask all guests to bring as many comic strips as possible (from newspapers).
- The host should collect the comics as the guests enter, then dress them in a humorous outfit using masking tape and newspaper. Give the guests accessories and makeup for completing their costume. Costumed guests can help host dress up the new arrivals.

Activities
- Divide into teams and hold a race to draw the best cartoon character. However, in order to get to the drawing board, each person must step only on comics (they should put one comic down, step on it, and then put another on the floor for their next step). Decide on a time limit before starting. This is done like a relay with each person on the team drawing for 30 seconds then coming back. First team to have a completed cartoon wins.
- When the end of the evening approaches, play charades.

317

College Mascot

Everyone must come dressed in their school colors, prepared to sing their school songs!

Activities
- Divide into teams. Have each person write three school trivia questions that they believe nobody can answer. The team who answers the most questions correctly wins the game.
- Play a game of softball or other group game.
- Play school band music in the background.

Menu
Serve make-your-own pizzas and beer (the main staples of college existence!).

318

Parent-Child Mural Painting Party

Design and paint a mural in a local school, a library, or other public building in need of sprucing up. Secure permission from appropriate authorities. Contact local artists for assistance.

Invitations
Send each family a copy of mural design. Ask them to bring paintbrushes and old clothes.

Activities
In designing the mural, use simple shapes and a theme to reflect local history and heritage. Use bright primary colors. Be sure to let all artists sign and date their masterpieces. Take photos to record the progress of the mural and artists.

Menu
Ask everyone to bring a dish to share. Make sure to have salads and desserts as well as main courses.

319

Blind Man's Bluff Mystery Party

Invitations
The invitations should be very brief, providing only the time and place of the party (or call invitations by telephone).

Decorations
Decorations depend on the place and theme of the party.

Activities
Arrange party at a mystery place such as a bowling alley, movie theatre, swimming club, tennis club, etc. Recruit enough drivers for transporting guests to party. When all guests have arrived, have a welcome drink and snacks. Have the drivers take different routes to confuse guests. Have a prize for the first guest who gueses the correct party location.

320

Board Game Party

Invitations
Use Monopoly play money, glue to a white piece of paper, and write party information on reverse.

Activities
Offer four different board games (of your choice). Set up games and have them ready to play for a predetermined length of time. Guests pick names out of a hat to see who they should play. The winners of each game should challenge each other.

Menu
Serve finger food throughout the evening, buffet style.

321

Stocks Going Up

Invitations
- Use a portion of a page from the stock section of a newspaper.
- Tear a hole in the center and glue it to a piece of paper. Write party information inside the ripped hole.
- Guests should come dressed in business suits.

Activities
- Cut out advertisements. Delete the word of the product. Hang them on the walls. Have guests guess the product names.
- Insider Information: Divide into teams and give each a company name. The teams should write a scandalous story about the company and then read their stories out loud.
- Under Our Suits: Place underwear, bras, long johns, sexy night-gowns, panty hose, etc. in a paper bag. Play music and pass the bag from guest to guest. When the music stops, the person must reach into the bag and select an item to put on over clothes. The person with the most garments on at the end of the specified time wins.

322

A Little Traveling Music, Please

This is a party your accountant will love...low cost and a great time. This party works well with a group of friends who have entertained together before. It is a good theme for beloved neighbors who are moving or for a new job promotion.

Invitations
• Invite guests to attend and host a portion of a traveling dinner party. The guests/party givers must plan menu and serve each course at a different home. After the food is served, everyone joins in and helps clean up!
• Dress should be formal.

Decorations
Place soft lights and candles on tables. Play romantic background music.

Menu
Ethnic menus are interesting. Allow guests to select their own recipes. The dinner should be four to five courses with each course at a different home. The guests should provide their own bottles of wine.

323

Tropical Paradise

Have you ever wondered what it's like to visit an island resort? Create one in your home or backyard! Guests should dress in resort clothes. Decorate the party area with green plants and flowers.

Activities
- Divide into partners.
- Give everyone a half-filled glass of water and a spoon.
- Blindfold the guests who are facing each other, and set a timer. The guests should feed each other spoonfuls of water simultaneously. The person with the least amount of water left wins the game.
- Hire a belly dancer or hula dancer to give everyone a lesson.

Menu
Serve barbequed chicken, fruit salads, and tarts.

324

You've Come a Long Way Baby

Have all guests bring a photograph of themselves as a baby and also as a teen. Guests should come dressed as something they have been in their past, for example, prom queen, pregnant, an athlete, mailman, tennis player, etc.

Activities
- Baby Dance: Divide baby pictures into male and female categories. Have each woman select the "baby" she wants as a dancing partner.
- Name That Tune: Collect hit records from the time period of high school for most of your guests. Divide into teams. The team with the most correct answers wins.
- Get a Clue: Have each person write three things about themselves on the back of their teenage picture. Stay in teams and read the first clue. Keep giving clues with the last clue being the picture. The team with the most correct answers wins the game.

325

Slide Party

This is a party for those who love to travel!

Invitations
- Draw or copy a globe to use as the invitation. Write party information on front.
- Ask guests to bring a tray of their favorite slides.

Decorations
- Decorate party area with maps and pictures from around the world.
- Set up a screen and a slide projector.

Activities
After socializing, start the show. Make sure that everyone says a little about their slides.

Menu
Serve appetizers from around the world.

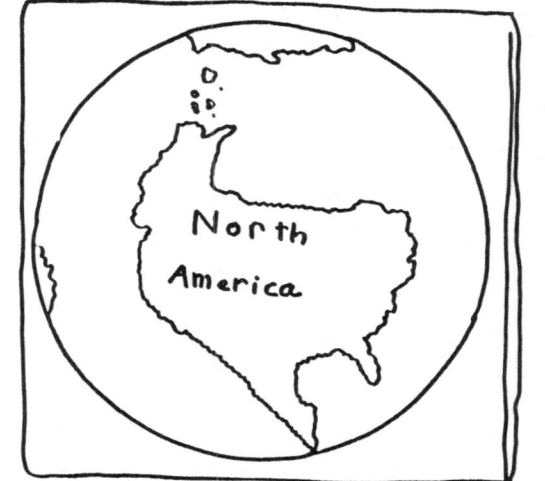

326

Newlywed Game

This is a great party for guests to get to know each other as couples. Not everyone has to be a contestant. You will need at least four sets of couples to answer questions. One couple must announce and everybody else is the audience.

Activities
Ask questions that might be funny and hard to remember, for example, "when and where was their first kiss?" and "what color is the wife's bathrobe?" Ask the women the questions first and have the men wait in another room where they can't hear the answers. Then, bring out the men and ask them to guess what their wives said. The same process should be done while asking the husbands the questions. Give a grand prize (such as a dinner for two) to the couple with the most points.

Menu
Serve desserts, coffee, tea, and hot chocolate.

327

Volunteer Tips

- Large events can take many hours to plan.
- Always appoint a volunteer coordinator and pull together a volunteer bank.
- Each committee/chairperson may call the bank and request helpers.
- Get children over ten years old involved (they are enthusiastic and full of energy).
- If you think you will need fifty volunteers, sign up one hundred, because one-third always drop out, and another group either doesn't show or forgets their assignments.

328

Invitation Know-How

- Invitations must not be scrimped on. Save money in other areas. The invitation must be unique and stand out. It is an indication of the fun and frolic to come.
- Donors are swamped by charity invitations. You should personalize the invitations perhaps by having committee members handwrite notes on them. Don't wait for an R.S.V.P.; follow-up with a phone call.

329

Sell Tickets and See Tickets Sell

Selling the ticket is the name of the game. Great public relations, volunteers, invitations, decorations, food, etc. will do nothing for your cause unless tickets are sold. Personal contact is the best method for selling a ticket. So, sell, sell, sell.

330

Raffle Ticket Tantalizers

Selling raffle tickets for raising funds is the oldest method known. Here are a few ideas for great prizes that will sell your tickets:

- cars
- vacation condos
- artwork
- health club memberships
- restaurant certificates
- cash awards
- service awards (prepare a gourmet dinner at your home, housecleaning, dinner with a local celebrity, etc.)
- boat cruises
- airline tickets
- clothing
- Ask a printer to donate tickets and ask travel agencies, restaurants, clubs, etc. for gift certificates (in exchange for a tax deduction).

331

Hello...Your Purchase Will Support...

Fund-raising sales that have proven to be successful for clubs and groups in the past are:

- pizza
- gift wrapping paper
- candy
- cookies
- fish fry
- dances
- services
- Christmas wreaths
- Christmas trees
- Christmas candy and cookies
- books and magazines
- coupon books
- sports tickets
- theatre tickets
- cookbooks
- cosmetics
- calendars

332

Waistline Fifties Dance

Invitations
• Use a fifties theme in making the invitations.
• The ticket takers have measuring tape and greet guests at door as they take their measurements.
• Admission for dance, which is based on the waistlines of the guests, is donated to charity. If a guest is shy about having their waist measured, have a set price to pay as an alternative.

Menu
Serve casual food out of booths, each offering a different item (hot dogs, pizza, French fries, etc.). Ask fast food restaurants to donate the food items.

333

Athletes on the Move

Theme
Progressive games for all the athletes in your group! Guests should wear athletic dress. It is best to hold this function at a country club or at a local Y.M.C.A. Select games that will take the same length of time and set a time limit for each.

Suggestions
• Basketball, racquetball, ping-pong, darts, swimming. Points are given to each first, second, and third place finisher. Guests purchase tickets to play each game. Guests can participate in as many events as they want.
• You will need many helpers.
• Hold a medal or trophy ceremony for overall winners.

Menu
Have a buffet available throughout the afternoon. Sell tickets for the purchase of food.

334

Boat Party

Rent a building such as a gym or a church that will have one large room and many small rooms. Decorate the party area to resemble a cruise ship with life preservers, travel posters, lounge chairs, etc. Use the large room for food and entertainment. Hire a local band for dance music.

Activities
- Room Ideas: A fitness room, where everybody must do a set of exercises; a spa, where guests receive a foot massage; a game room, with board and trivia games; etc.
- Divide into groups. As you ring a bell, each group moves into a different room.

335

Cruise for Charity

Arrange with a local river or lake cruising company to rent or loan you a boat for a brunch or dinner excursion. If you must rent the boat, charge extra for the tickets. Hire a band for dancing. This event takes hard work but it is worth it. It can also become an annual event.

336

Box Supper Auction and Dance

This event is best when done with a group who is familiar with one another, such as a church or school.

- The ladies should bring box suppers in decorated containers which are auctioned off to the highest bidder (you will need an auctioneer for this).
- Hire a band for polkas or square dancing.

337

Cakewalk

- Appoint a committee to call people to donate cakes.
- Determine the amount of money you want to raise and the number of cakes needed.
- Arrange a hall or a place to hold the cakewalk.
- Hire a live band.
- Display cakes on tables.
- Make a maypole with many long ribbons. Each ribbon has a piece of paper attached with "your prize is..." or "no prize" written on it.
- Participants purchase tickets, each for a ribbon on the maypole.

Activities

The cakewalk is played just like musical chairs is played. The ticket holders take hold of the ribbons that they purchased. As the music plays, the contestants weave in and out around the pole. When music stops, the winner is the person standing on a target that is taped to the floor. Each winner picks any cake they wish from the table. The game continues until all the cakes are chosen.

338

Christmas in Summertime

This is a Christmas party where deprived children and adults receive gifts. The party is held during the summer with a focus on a particular agency. Ask the needy for a "wish list" and a "needs list." Send the lists with the invitations, so guests will know what gifts to bring and whom they are for.

Invitations
The invitation should resemble a Christmas symbol such as a tree, a sleigh, Santa Claus, etc.

Decorations
- Have Christmas gift wrapping paper, ribbons, and cards available for guests to use for gifts, a Christmas tree, and ornaments for children to hang.
- Play Christmas music.
- Have someone dressed up as Santa to give children their presents.

Menu
Serve Christmas cookies and punch.

339

Christmas Bazaar

- Hold a committee meeting by Labor Day to select booths and assign duties.
- Hang flyers and posters in prominent places around the community the day following Thanksgiving.
- Reserve a location for the bazaar well ahead of time.
- Each booth committee uses Christmas decorations and plays tapes of caroling and other Christmas music in each booth.

Booth Suggestions
- Information booth with maps.
- Santa booth for photos.
- Christmas mail booth with stamps, wrappings, etc.
- Mother's booth with gifts for mom.
- Father's booth for gifts for dad.
- Expensive tastes booth with top-of-the-line items such as Dom Perignon, etc.
- Children's booth with gifts for all ages.
- Book lovers' booth with all types of novels, etc.

340

Christmas Wrapping Paper Sale

- Christmas wrapping paper can be sold at a high mark-up, and can be purchased wholesale at a bulk rate.
- Door-to-door sales work well when held in early November.
- Birthday, wedding, and other gift wrapping paper can be offered throughout the year.

341

Family Walk-a-Thon

This is a good event for supporting a neighborhood cause. Plan a route for the walk and print maps and posters. Select local businesses and restaurants for donations.

- Families must sign up and find their own sponsors at set amounts of money.
- Other "thon" ideas include cycling, jumping rope, skating, swimming, reading, and almost anything else!

Menu
Hold a family picnic at a local park following the event and hold an awards ceremony. Reserve the space ahead of time.

342

Monte Carlo Magnifique

Invitations
- Write or print information on a card in the shape of a top hat with a silver background.
- Reserve a country club in advance.
- Hire coatroom helpers and valet parkers.
- Hire a band for dancing, but be certain to listen to their demo tape first.
- Meet with caterers in advance and plan menu.

Decorations
- Fill the party room with black, white, and silver balloons.
- Table centerpieces should be fresh flowers with black and white accents. Spray some of the flowers with silver paint.
- Give a long-stemmed red rose to each female guest and a red rose boutonniere to the gentlemen.

Menu
Serve quenelles of walleye pike in watercress sauce with Russian caviar, fresh Maine lobsters, seasonal fresh vegetables, wild rice with grapes, cherries flambé, red and white wine with dinner, and champagne with dessert.

343

Plant and Flower Sale

This event is best when held in early April. Contact florists and nurseries to sell plants to your organization at a wholesale price. Prepare posters and flyers and distribute by March 1st. The posters should feature the plants and flowers that will be sold. Hold the sale at a central location such as a school, park, or church. Have plenty of order blanks available with a tear-off portion detailing the plant pick-up date, time, and place. It is best not to offer to deliver the plants, as this will eat up your profits. This is good for Mother's Day or Valentine's Day.

344

Tennis or Golf Celebrity Tourney

Recruit several celebrities who are willing to play in your charity event.
Reserve courts or golf course well in advance. Solicit prizes from local
businesses. Sell tickets to people who would like to play golf and tennis
with a celebrity. End the day with dinner or snacks.

345

Singles Dance Auction

Begin planning event well in advance. Hold event in a club or bar with a live disc jockey. Arrange with the club or bar to receive a percentage of bar receipts. Pre-sell tickets in advance. Solicit singles to be offered at auction for dances. Try to recruit a local celebrity for M.C. Have the D.J. or M.C. auction singles before each dance.

Auction Format
- Have printed program with numbered biography on each single to be auctioned. Give single same number to carry on-stage as M.C. is narrating his/her biography.
- Individuals in audience then bid on single of their choice. Bidding can start at given amount of money.

346

Fashion Fun

This is a fashion show luncheon. It is fun for the "models" as well as the watchers.

• Find a clothing store that will donate outfits for the fashion show. Make sure the style of the clothes fit the personality of the women in your group who will be doing the modeling.

• Reserve a place to have the show. You don't have to have a runway. Models can walk casually around the room, from table to table.

• Try to enlist the help of local celebrities as the M.C. or as models. Wives of professional athletes are ideal to work with because their names will help sell tickets and they already function as a group.

• Sell tickets and practice!

347

Valentine Kiss-a-Gram Dance

Hold the party at a school gym. The boys and girls can request that a kiss-a-gram be sent to their "sweetheart" for $1.00 for a designated charity. Everybody dances in gym while the kiss-a-grams are being delivered.

Invitations

Spread the word around that you are hosting a special type of Valentine's party on February 14th. Arrange to have three boys and three girls ready to deliver "kiss-a-gram" invitations to the dates of the guests you know will be invited. Dance tickets can be purchased and presented to the person of your choice for a dance. The tickets should be made in the shape of a heart. The person collecting the most hearts at the end of the evening is the sweetheart king or queen.

Decorations

Decorate gym with red, pink, and white balloons, crepe paper, streamers, Cupid cut-outs and large cardboard hearts suspended by nylon fishing line from the ceiling. Have a white trellis archway and decorate with roses. This is a good background for a Polaroid photo booth.

348

Vanishing Tea Parties

Enlist the help of a few of your friends who will donate an agreed amount of money when they attend a hosted tea. For example, six to ten women should meet at an afternoon tea, make a set donation of $10-$20 and then agree to hold their own tea and invite six different friends. The process of having one tea the first week, six the second, twelve the third, etc. will bring in a lot of donation money! The hostess is responsible for collecting the donations from her guests and turning them in to her chairperson. She must also follow up by encouraging her guests to have their own tea parties the following week. If you want to do this on a larger scale, hold a larger initial tea party.

349

Party Planning

Start planning a month ahead. Answer these questions:

- Reason for celebration?
- What does guest of honor like or dislike? When will they be available?
- Decide the best place to hold the party. In the home or outside the home?
  Budget will help to determine many of the decisions. If held outside the home in an
  entertainment place or restaurant, party room, etc., call and make reservations early.
- Best day of the week? Best time? How long should party last?
- Prepare guest lists.
- Mentally walk through party from guests' arrival to departure.
- Review safety factors of your party area.
- Pretend you are the guest. What would you enjoy or expect?
- Select party theme or motif.
- Check pages 357 through 365 in this book for further information on
  specific age groups and ideas best suited to them.

350

Continued next page

Party Planning (cont.)

- Decide on invitations and date to mail to guests.
- Start menu plans depending on theme, time of day, number of guests, and budget.
- Prepare shopping lists. 1-food, perishables, 2-beverages, 3-decorations, 4-non-perishables, 5-paper needs.
- Will you prepare all the menu or will you enlist friends or a caterer to help?
- Prepare a list of "helpers" on the party day to add extra hands that will be needed.
- If you decide on outside caterer, call several and interview several before deciding which one will best suit your needs and budget. They offer a wide range of services.
- Look through book to get fresh new ideas.
- Keep album of celebration ideas and invitations you have been sent or have seen.

351

What Helpers Can Do and When

Ask party helpers to arrive one hour early so you may explain the help you will need and who will help in each area. Let them know you appreciate their help. If you are having fifteen or more children and/or adults, you will need a minimum of three helpers. Having one of the helpers be a licensed car driver is often a big help in case of an emergency. Some areas needing help are as follows:

- Children's parties - aid with coat and boot removal.
- Adult parties - hanging up coats on arrival.
- Hosting new arrivals while party hosts and guest of honor answer the door.
- Escorting guests to party area and/or bathroom or telephone.
- If party is being videotaped: taking video pictures as guests arrive and/or play the games, open gifts, during cake presentation.
- Being in charge of the music played in the background and changing tapes or CD's.
- During cake presentation and gift opening.

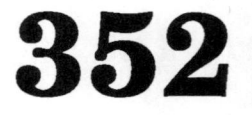

352

Continued next page

What Helpers Can Do and When (cont.)

- Helping with the serving of the party menu. Serving and filling plates in the kitchen or on party tables. Setting the table pre-party.
- Cleaning up spills: assisting party guests with refills and needs that may arise.
- If birthday, take care of lights during cake presentation time. Hold door open for cake entry.
- Let party helpers know where party supplies, bathroom supplies, emergency needs are kept.
- Siblings are a big help at parties. If siblings feel useful at the party they will have a feeling of self esteem and you will not encounter some of the jealousy they might otherwise feel.
- Family animals which live in house should be kept away from the party area.

353

Parties Outside the Home

Having a party outside the home places some limits on your control of the party and its movement.

Find out if you can do the following:

- Set up the party area as you like. Set up the table, or eat on the floor (for small guests)
- Have a group entrance or private showing.
- Bring in your own refreshments and/or cake.
- What must you supply? Plates, napkins, utensils, etc.
- Is there an area for group to meet privately after event?
- Ask question up front about the limitations there may be at location you have chosen.
- Is there parking or a bus available?

354

Parties in Restaurants

- Try and find a room that will be private for your party guests and not in public traffic plan.
- Call first and go look at the party area to be used.
- Do not make all plans by phone or by someone else's recommendation sight unseen. Your party is entirely different.
- Find out the least busy day.

Some things to check when making final arrangements:
- Is there a restroom near your room?
- Can you move the furniture around to set up the room to match your party's needs and theme?
- Make sure room is not too large or guests may get "lost" in it. Be sure the room is bright.
- What is the general atmosphere of the room?
  Is the fee reasonable?

355

Unique and Unseen Party Places

If your home doesn't seem to fit the appropriate party theme, try one of these unique and unseen party places. Make sure you call in advance and find out all the rules, costs, what you need to supply, whether food and drinks are allowed, etc.

- bakeries
- post offices
- pumpkin farms
- farms
- newspaper printer
- pizza parlor
- candy factory
- costume tailor
- set designing studio

- museums
- puppet theaters
- live theaters
- boat cruise
- movie theater
- rodeo
- miniature golf course
- bowling lanes
- sporting events

- concert or play
- swimming pool
- gym
- circus
- movie studio
- T.V. station
- skating rinks
- zoos

- Most importantly, use your imagination. These are just some suggestions you might want to try. Be creative, and don't forget to check for local information in your phone book.

One Year Olds

The party is for the parents, relatives, and friends at this age. Do not frighten or overload the "special day." Only have 3 to 4 other babies, with their parents. Shorter is sweeter for this age. One hour to one hour and a half at most. A brunch or lunch for adult guests set from 11:30 to 12:30, or dessert and beverages from 4 to 5. Between or after babies' naps will ensure a happy celebration for all. Two extra helpers will be smart at all toddlers' parties. Do not expect parents or relatives to "help." They will have their hands full.

357

Two Year Olds

Terrible twos was never more evident as at a two year old party. Make sure every guest has their parent or a one-on-one supervisor at all times. Twos do not have attention spans or focus for entertainment, structured events, or group activity. They enjoy the fun around the table, the cake, and not much more. Do not be disappointed in this reaction. 4 to 8 guests with adults or baby-sitters is the most to invite. Do not invite older siblings or friends. Twos do not mix well. One hour is the time limit to stick to. Best of luck!

358

Three Year Olds

This age can enjoy a party with others. They are beginning to socialize in a party atmosphere. Me, Me, Me can stop for a while when they see friends and choose to join the fun and the short directions for an easy-to-do activity. They will laugh and feel part of the party. Only invite three year olds for the most successful party. Threes like threes. 8 to 12 guests with three adult helpers will work. Most threes do not like to be left alone at the party, but are happy if parent is in the other room. One hour to one hour and a half is tops for their short attention span and short sharing time. They need to be awake and alert to enjoy the party. Lunch or late afternoon cake and ice cream is best. If your child has a favorite story or short game use it. Taped background music should be children's tape or soft, low music. This is true for all children's parties regardless of age.

359

Four Year Olds

They are great party goers and havers. . . the party starts as they enter preschool circles. They look forward to their own birthday and parties months ahead and want to help pick the guests and activities. Ask the child who they want to invite. They have definite ideas. They have a longer sharing and attention span time now and more self-control due to more school and other group functions. 9-14 guests will make a nice number. Parents may now drop the invited child off and leave. More helpers are required since this is the case. Time should be one to two hours from noon to 6 pm. Most depends on the entertainment and/or activities. After 5-6 pm, these party animals will slow down and want to be home with Mommy and Daddy.

360

Five Year Olds

What an age for parties! Great guests and great hosts, fives have a wonderful sense of humor and enjoy parties to the fullest. Invite 12 to 15 guests. Fives are very independent. Their parents may drop them off and pick them up after the party. However, they may not want the party to end. Party can last anywhere from one and a half to two hours successfully. Make sure to have carefully structured and scheduled games and activities. Walk through party schedule before party day. One or two party helpers are a must. Ask your child who they want to invite. Fives usually want boys and girls and will not insist guests are from the same school or know each other. Age-geared activities work best. Include your child in the picking of theme, invitations, and activities.

361

Six Year Olds

Sixes enjoy lively, high-spirited parties. Extra party helpers may be a good idea. Invite at least 16 to 20 guests. Sixes will be comfortable with five year olds and young seven year olds. Active games and scheduling extra events are important. Sixes move quickly from game to game and can finish quicker than you can tell them the rules. Be forewarned. Ask child who they want to invite and the type of party they want to have. Sixes will want to be very involved in pre-party planning from invitations to picking the food and cake. For sixes this is the best part of the party. Length of party can vary but two hours is the longest. Sixes are a good age to have parties outside the home or a "tour type" party due to new school experiences of group activities.

362

Seven Year Olds

Ask your child how they feel about the party. Who do they want to have attend? Most want a party with lots of friends. Like sixes, sevens want to help plan every moment of their party. Pre-party planning is fun but sevens continue to build the excitement at the party. Most sevens prefer a special event outside the home, for example, movies, theater, puppet show, zoo, or ice skating rink. Easy as it sounds, outside the home parties take much advance work. Go to the party site, walk through the party, and time the schedule to avoid disasters. Because the schedule is important, it helps if it is written out and in a place easy to view. From the time the first guest is greeted at the front door it is paramount that the guests know who is in charge, the party schedule, and the rules of behavior. If you state this clearly in the beginning of the party, you and the guests will enjoy the party. Set firm ground rules. Best party behavior is expected.

363

Eight Year Olds

All these suggestions are general; you know your child best. This age group has specific ideas about what they want and do not want. Listen to your child. They may not want a party. This is O.K. They usually feel more comfortable with fewer close friends. A special activity or event may be what your child desires. Let your child direct you. Surprise parties at this age are usually a bomb. A professional sports event, theater event, or new movie may be the ticket. "Slumber parties" or sleep-overs are popular at these ages. Even though the party may last a longer time, the essence of the party must be well planned. Eating time and cake presentation should still be a "wow" event for the guest of honor. Extra helpers are necessary. Fathers are great!

364

Early and Late Teens

Early teens like to be involved in planning their party's theme, guest lists, and especially type and amount of food to be served. Some like surprise parties; others are embarrassed by them. Surprise parties work best if given by friends of teen. If you decide on a surprise, consult teen's friends for guest list. Outings away from the home reflecting the teen's hobbies and interests offer new party environments.

Late teens feel they are maturing and are more grown up. They tend to think parties are "kid stuff" but still enjoy partying. Many late teens hold parties when parents are gone. It is important to communicate with your teens regarding their feelings and yours about parties without parents, and parties with alcohol and drug use. Let them know you share their concern regarding peer pressure and parties. Be firm but supportive.

365

Index

Teen Birthdays Con't.

PGA Miniature Golf Party, **60**
Pizza Party with a Twist, **61**
Couples Crazy Valentine Party, **62**
Detective Party, **63**
Soap Opera Surprise, **64**
Dance Party, **65**
Star Search, **66**
Pajama Party, **67**
Me and My Mime Party, **68**
A Day in Court, **69**

Adult Birthdays

Marathon Birthday Party, **70**
Bean Party, **71**
Surprise Birthday for Me, **72**
Women's Bridge Party, **73**
On the Spot Party, **74**
Hello to Hollywood, **75**
Husband's Reign Stag Party, **76**
Fabulous Forties Birthday Party, **77**
I Lost Track of Time, **78**
Man of the Year, **79**
Surprise Workout Party, **80**

Top of Parking Lot Party, **81**
Surprise Slumber Party, **82**
Let's Flip Our Wigs, **83**
Mixing Business with Pleasure, **84**
Tailgate Birthday Celebration, **85**
King for a Night, **86**
Bocce Ball Birthday, **87**
Turn About Birthday, **88**
Rib Tickler Party, **89**
Fifties Fantasy Sock Hop, **90**

Showers for New Parents

The ABC's of Motherhood, **91**
Pink and Blue, **92**
Sibling Shower, **93**
The Way We Were, **94**
Chosen One, **95**
Carpenters' Convention, **96**
Day at the Spa, **97**
Stork Shower, **98**
New Mothers Welcome to
Neighborhood Party, **99**
Share a Book, **100**
End of Your Personal Life, **101**
Weight Watching Party, **102**

Career Fair, **103**
Mother Goose, **104**
Gifts for Mother, **105**
Nursery "Deco" Party, **106**
What Child is This?, **107**
Pass it On, **108**
Baby First Aid, **109**
Second Chance, **110**
Learn Baby Massage, **111**

Wedding and Personal Showers

Rock Around the Clock, **112**
Couch Potato Shower, **113**
Lean on Me Shower, **114**
So They Eloped, **115**
Wine and Cheese Shower, **116**
Be My Valentine Shower, **117**
Breakfast Shower, **118**
Picnic Barbeque Shower, **119**
Cookbook Shower, **120**
Honeymoon Shower, **121**
Couple's Kitchen Shower, **122**
Gift Display Get Together, **123**
Garden Tea Shower, **124**